T0309007

Nina Christensen
Charlotte Appel

Children's Literature

in the Nordic World

Aarhus University Press / The University of Wisconsin Press

The Nordic World
Children's Literature in the Nordic World
© Nina Christensen and Charlotte Appel 2021

Cover, layout, and typesetting:
Camilla Jørgensen, Trefold
Cover photograph: Stine Rasmussen and
Montgomery
Copy editors: Heidi Flegal and Mia Gaudern
Acquisitions editors: Amber Rose Cederström
and Karina Bell Ottosen
This book is typeset in FS Ostro and printed
on Munken Lynx 130 g
Printed by Narayana Press, Denmark
Printed in Denmark 2021

ISBN 978 87 7219 591 9
ISBN 978 0 299 33634 9

This book is available in a digital edition

Library of Congress Cataloging-in-Publication
data is available

Published with the generous support of the
Aarhus University Research Foundation,
the Carlsberg Foundation and the Nordic
Council of Ministers

The Nordic World series is copublished by
Aarhus University Press and the University
of Wisconsin Press

Aarhus University Press
aarhusuniversitypress.dk

The University of Wisconsin Press
uwpress.wisc.edu

PEER
REVIEWED

MIX
Paper
FSC FSC® C010651

Contents

Chapter 1.

Introduction

This book is about children's literature and the reading cultures of children in the Nordic countries from around 1750 up to today. With Denmark as the main example, we trace the variety of texts, genres, and media encountered by different children; what they did with their books; how books were linked to other media; and how children and adults interacted in relation to literature and education. One key ambition is to show the variety in children's 'literary diet', drawing attention to the fact that Nordic children have always experienced narratives in combinations of written, oral, visual, and performed texts, and that they have never just read the books explicitly written and published for them, nor only read the literature originating in their own countries. For these reasons, this is not a history of children's literature that focuses on selected authors and their works written specifically for children.[1]

Our book is divided into chapters roughly covering the periods 1750–1820, 1820–1900, 1900–1950, 1950–2000, and the early twenty-first century. We open each chapter with two or three short cases, following individual children and exploring the reading and media cultures of their environments and of their times. Each chapter also identifies and describes important societal contexts, not least devel-

1. The most recent overview of children's literature in the Nordic countries in English is Westin (2004). Heikkilä-Halttunen (2012) addresses tendencies in Finnish children's literature after 1980. Weinreich (2006), Birkeland et al. (2018), Kristjánsdóttir (2015), and Zweigbergk (1965) provide overviews of the history of Danish, Norwegian, Icelandic, and Swedish children's literature, respectively

opments in schools, education, and changing conceptions of childhood. Throughout, we introduce selected examples of children's literature – both old and new, and either written in or translated into Nordic languages – and examples of books combined with other media. Thus, composite chronologies will be woven into the fabric of this account.

We present the reading cultures of specific children in order to highlight children's varied *practices* in their use of books and media. Furthermore, these miniature portraits point to the interplay between children's own priorities, influential adults in their lives, and the development of institutions like schools and libraries. A range of differences among children will appear from our accounts of boys and girls, children from poor and rich families, and those from rural and urban environments. The memoirs and autobiographies used as sources for these cases are often written by men and women who became authors later in life, and the children from poor backgrounds may well be described as pattern-breakers. Their experiences are hardly typical, but precisely because they took an interest in literature as adults, they have written about their childhoods and their – often limited – access to books and other media.[2] Read across centuries, these cases provide glimpses not only into differences between children living in certain periods, but also into changes and remarkable continuities among generations of Nordic children.

A number of books read by children in Denmark and other Nordic countries from about 1750 to 2020 will be presented, with a focus on genres and titles that were widely read at their time. Some were written by Nordic authors while others were published as translations or adaptations of international literature. While attention will be paid to new trends in terms of medium, content, and form – such as the development of picturebooks from the 1840s, Astrid Lindgren's novels about the highly independent Pippi Longstocking in the 1940s, or the publication of

2. On the methodologies involved in following specific children through autobiographical sources, see Appel et al. (forthcoming)

8

children's own humorous and grotesque texts in the 1970s – we also point to the longevity of certain genres, and to a number of titles that became steady sellers and were adapted to new media through several decades or even centuries.[3] Special attention will be paid to the development – and the consistencies – of the *codex*, that is, the 'classic' book consisting of inscribed pages sewn or glued together and surrounded by a binding.

Based on these intentions, our study is interdisciplinary in its approach, drawing on theories and methods from comparative literature, cultural history, childhood studies, and book history. Our interest in interactions between adults and children has been particularly inspired by "the kinship model", presented by the American scholar Marah Gubar (2016). Gubar encourages focus on the interaction and the similarities between adults and children, as well as increased attention on the heterogeneity and varied development of individual children. This offers an alternative to earlier descriptions of childhood as a progressive development through certain stages, ending up with a transition from child, defined by difference or deficit, to adult.[4] Moreover, she suggests scholars consider children as active participants in producing and molding the texts and media they use.

Inevitably, children's use of books and media is related to adults' wishes to interact with children as present and future individuals. The aim of such interactions can – in various combinations – be education, entertainment, play, or aesthetic experiences created for, with, and not least by children. In this regard, a second strand of our scholarly inspiration comes from a consideration of children's *agency*, defined as their possibility and right to act independently and exert influence on their own life circumstances – including when it comes to books and media.[5] This approach is linked to our focus on practices, and we attempt to highlight agency among adult actors, too.

3. For in-depth analyses of Nordic children's literature, see, for instance, the Nordic journals *Barnboken* and *Barnelitterært forskningstidsskrift / Nordic Journal of ChildLit Aesthetics*, also available online

4. For a brief discussion of the concept *child*, see James & James (2012): 14–16. For definitions of this term in a historical context, see entries in Fass et al. (2004); specifically in relation to Denmark and the Nordic region, see Coninck-Smith (2021)

5. For recent discussions of *agency* as a concept and an approach, see Maza (2020), Christensen (2021), and Coninck-Smith & Appel (2021)

Therefore, alongside authors of children's literature, the readers of this book will find parents and relatives, teachers and publishers, booksellers and other professionals, as well as children's friends and schoolmates.

When tracing individual children, we are led to children's frequent cross-media practices. This interest in individual *media repertoires*, tapping into available *media ensembles* of different environments, has been inspired by methodologies and concepts developed in recent media research (Hasebrink & Hepp 2017). To study such phenomena historically, we use a wide range of sources. We study not only specific or "proper" children's literature, but also other books and media used by children, going beyond the texts themselves by including the illustrations, paratexts,[6] and materialities of children's media. Moreover, we include sources such as diaries, letters, autobiographies, advertisements, commercial and scholarly reports, and national statistics.

This variety of sources also springs from our wish to embed the account of children's literature in broader cultural and historical contexts. Political changes and new social and economic developments have influenced children's access to literature and media. In addition, many changes and events have emerged as central topics in children's books and media. Legal changes that affect school attendance, for instance, or the development of institutions such as libraries and daycare facilities, interact closely with children's use of media and the market for children's books. In the following chapters, we also give examples of how religious, political, and social movements such as eighteenth-century pietism, nineteenth-century nationalism, and new gender roles in the late twentieth century have influenced reading traditions, media production, and the form and contents of specific works.

Historical contexts are, inevitably, highly specific. In this book on Nordic children's literature, which covers

6. Following Gérard Genette (1997), we use the word "paratexts" to refer to a variety of texts surrounding and presenting the main text, such as title pages, prefaces, advertisements, etc.

7. For a general outline in English of Danish history since 1750, see Jespersen (2011) and Borring Olesen & Poulsen (forthcoming). For a history of the entire Nordic region, see Gustafsson (2017)

almost three centuries and intends to highlight changes as well as continuities, we have chosen to use Denmark as our main case or our key example, so that historical contexts and developments can be explained more easily along the way.[7] Children's literature from other Nordic countries, mainly Norway, Sweden, and the Swedish-speaking parts of Finland, will also be included, not least because the three Scandinavian languages (Danish, Norwegian, and Swedish) are closely related, meaning that translations, cooperation, and exchanges are frequent. Other articles and books have addressed the idea of a particular "Nordic childhood", which – as far as children's literature is concerned – has been associated with characteristics like a general readiness to speak openly to children about sex, death, and other previously taboo-affected topics (Ommundsen 2015; Øster 2016). On a more general or societal level, researchers have related "Nordic childhood" to a willingness to listen to – and respect – children's own opinions on matters both private and public, and to the existence of rights, institutions, and organizations that promote and secure children's democratic participation in society (Brembeck et al. 2004; Faye Jacobsen 2017). While including elements of what might be specific Nordic features in our account of children's literature and reading cultures in the Nordic world, contrasting these with other countries or regions lies beyond the scope of this book.

Instead, the following chapters will address the strong and complex interactions between national, Nordic, and international texts and contexts that relate to children's literature, and also point to cases where Nordic cooperation has been strong and influential. Above all, however, this book is an alternative account of children's literature, with its focus on children's reading cultures and media use as a practice. We hope that, in its very concentrated form, it can serve as an introduction for everyone who has an interest in children's literature, as an inspiration in classrooms internationally, and as a point of departure for further investigations into differences and similarities across the Nordic region and beyond.

En skolestue (A Schoolroom)
Painting by Peter Cramer (undated, c. 1760-1770).
© Private collection

Chapter 2.
Educating young hearts and minds, 1750-1820

The late decades of the eighteenth century witnessed the emergence of new kinds of children's books and media in the Nordic region. These new commodities were mainly available to middle- and upper-class children in the cities, while children from less privileged backgrounds primarily encountered a small curriculum of religious books at school, but had the opportunity to access more books and media, for instance when finding or producing texts themselves. Around 1800, some publishers began to specialize in children's books that provided education as well as entertainment. In many texts the child was addressed as a potentially enlightened citizen, and much fiction introduced the child to characters representing vices and virtues.

Hans Christian and Friederike

The Danish-German author Friederike Brun (1765-1835) and the Danish fairytale author Hans Christian Andersen (1805-1875) exemplify the huge differences between rich and poor children in their access to education and books during this period. What they share is a strong interest in a variety of texts, and a strong inclination to perform and entertain.

It is possible to get an impression of a poor boy's reading culture in the early nineteenth century by studying the autobiographies of Hans Christian Andersen. He grew up in the provincial city of Odense as the son of a shoemaker. In their humble home, the boy and his parents slept in the same room, where many daily activities also took place: working, cooking, sleeping, playing – and reading. The author stresses the aesthetic aspects: "The walls, however, were covered with pictures; on the chest of drawers there were some pretty cups, glasses and bric-a-brac, and above my father's bench there was a shelf containing books and songs" (Andersen 2013: 14). Andersen recalls how his father would often read aloud from comedies by the Norwegian-Danish playwright Ludvig Holberg, *The Arabian Nights*, or a novel by the German author August Lafontaine. He also describes how oral narratives were a constant source of entertainment in his home, and how old women would tell stories in the streets and in the asylum for the poor and the sick, which he sometimes visited with his grandmother. When he and his mother went to the countryside to visit old friends, their ghost stories would scare him out of his wits.

Hans Christian learned the alphabet from an elderly woman who made a living teaching small children elementary literacy. Later, at school, his teacher gave vivid and inspiring renditions of stories from the Bible, and when he got older, a pastor's widow took an interest in him and invited him into her home, where books from a lending library were read aloud. Here, he was also introduced to Shakespeare, who became a great inspiration for the boy when he performed plays with the toy theater his father had made for him.

Hans Christian became an entertainer at a very young age and was invited to sing in wealthy people's homes. His mother sent him to work at a factory, but disliking the labor he started to sing and tell stories so that his colleagues would let him perform for them instead. Judging from Andersen's memoirs – which of course tend to underscore this aspect – in his childhood it was a huge pleasure for him to write his own pieces of drama and read them aloud, and his main activities and ambitions were to seek out, find, absorb, and reproduce fiction of any sort. After his confirmation, Hans Christian, now 14, longed to go to the Danish capital, where he knew there was a larger and better theater. He left home, made his way to Copenhagen on a one-way ticket he had bought with the money he had earned from entertaining, and began his struggle to move upwards in society.

The meager resources and limited access to books in Hans Christian Andersen's home provide a stark contrast to the experiences of Friederike Brun, as described in her autobiography. Friederike grew up in a privileged family as a daughter of the German pastor at the large St Petri Church in Copenhagen. Around 1800 she became an author and hosted a prominent literary salon at her estate outside Copenhagen. In her autobiography she describes herself as a witty and independent girl who learned to read at the age of four. One of her father's friends, the famous German educator Johann Bernhard Basedow (1724-1790), suggested making her an alphabet out of tasty cakes, and she ate it "with such heartfelt joy and in such exaggeration that it became necessary to interfere with the delight she took in learning" (Brun 1824: 15).[8]

After receiving the most basic instruction, Friederike had to educate herself. She began by reading German translations of popular novels by the English author Samuel Richardson, such as *Pamela* (1740), *Clarissa* (1748), and *The History of Sir Charles Grandison* (1753). She read

8. This and all of the subsequent translations (of book titles and quotations) are by the authors of this text. Unless otherwise stated, the year of publication refers to the first edition in the relevant language

while rocking the cradle of her younger sister and admits that she only understood one-tenth of these popular epistolary novels (Brun 1824: 25). In 1824, when she published her autobiography, books printed for children had become common and popular, in contrast to during her childhood, when "little was written for children, and what was there would almost always bore me" (29). Today, the fiction she read, such as the fables by the German author Christian F. Gellert, might be considered *crossover fiction*, of the type read by children and adults alike.

At the age of seven, Friederike got a room of her own, and she had more opportunities than most girls concerning what, where, and when to read. When she was ten, her father gave her the keys to his library and his study. There, among other books, she could read and contemplate the compilation of poems and copperplates representing "famous German men" that kindled her desire to produce poetry herself. Like Hans Christian, the young Friederike often transformed the stories she read into drama, which she would perform with friends and relatives. They did their own version of *Clarissa*, and when she and her family visited the influential Danish nobleman and politician Christian Ditlev Reventlow (1748-1824) on his estate, she directed *Grandison*, with Count Reventlow himself playing the main character (Brun 1824: 115). At home, she and her brothers enacted scenes from a play by the Danish author Johannes Ewald in a nearby garden. Friederike clearly liked to entertain, and she describes how other children were placed in her care, even when she was still quite young, because she knew so many fairytales by heart.

The level of detail and the pride and joy Brun invests in recounting her many literary and cultural activities mark a contrast to her very brief mention of the limited education provided by her father. While her brother was given a private tutor, she was left to her own devices. Her brother's tutor taught her writing and a bit of Latin, but her father rebuffed her desire to learn Latin systematically, saying: "I will not have her made into a scholarly fool" (Brun 1824: 32). Friederike Brun ends a chapter of her autobiography with these words, thereby encouraging her reader to contemplate the (deficient) wisdom of this decision. Even though she had access to more knowledge and more media than most other children of her day, there were clearly limits to the education of a privileged girl, compared to boys of the same social standing.

Instruction in reading and religion

Despite varieties in children's reading cultures depending on their social background and gender, certain general characteristics are identifiable in children's literacy and reading in the Nordic region during the latter half of the eighteenth century. All Nordic countries were predominantly agricultural societies, with 80-95% of the population living in rural areas, and all had been Lutheran since the reformations of the sixteenth century. Around 1750, the vast majority of Nordic boys and girls received some sort of elementary schooling with instruction in Christian doctrines and basic literacy – the skill of reading printed books in the vernacular. Clergymen had long advocated initial training in functional literacy as a way for children to learn Luther's catechism by heart. In Sweden most clergymen could not carry out such teaching themselves, due to the widely scattered settlements, and the Swedish Church Law of 1686 had explicitly made parents responsible for teaching their children to read at home.[9] In contrast, most Danish children were taught in some sort of school, organized by the clergy, the village community, or local schoolteachers, often in collaboration. Teaching small children to read printed text could be a means to earn a living for widows, disabled soldiers, elderly people, or young boys with no family to support them, so potential teachers were available in most places. Across the Nordic

9. On the practices and results of Swedish home schooling, see Johansson (1981) and Graff et al. (2009). Home schooling was prevalent in large parts of Norway too

region, children's schooling was organized in many different ways, depending on gender, social conditions, urban or rural setting, and other factors. Some children, mainly boys from relatively prosperous families, were also taught writing and mathematics, and a minority of boys went to traditional grammar schools that gave instruction in Latin (Appel & Coninck-Smith, vol. 1, 2013–2015).

The practical teaching methods and the books they employed were largely the same in all Nordic countries. Children would learn to recognize letters by looking at the alphabet printed on the first page of an "ABC": an inexpensive, often unbound primer, usually consisting of 16 pages in octavo format.[10] Sometimes the alphabet page was glued onto a small wooden board with a handle, called a "hornbook". Following the alphabet, a page or two would contain short combinations of consonants and vowels to train spelling. Next, the child would find three well-known Christian texts – the Lord's Prayer, the Ten Commandments, and the Creed – often with all words hyphenated at each syllable. Most children already knew the wording, which was supposed to make it easier for them to crack the code of reading. Because of the ABC's contents and function as the first step in the religious curriculum, this booklet can be described as a *catechism primer*.[11] Like other Nordic books in the vernacular, the ABC was printed in Gothic typeface. These letters were called "Danish letters" (or "Swedish letters"), in contrast to the Antiqua or "Latin letters" used for scholarly publications.

Once children had begun to read properly, they would move on to their second book: Luther's *Small Catechism* of approximately 80 pages. In this book, the children encountered Luther's voice as they worked their way through his explanations of the above-mentioned three texts, each with its own part in the catechism, plus additional parts on baptism, communion, and – often – the so-called table-of-duties. This last element was a brief guide

10. An octavo is a book made out of paper sheets folded three times, so that each sheet creates eight pages or, when printed on both sides, 16 pages in all. Most ABCs were made out of a single sheet. Larger formats (folios and quartos, with sheets folded once or twice) required more paper and were therefore more expensive. Some books were printed in even smaller formats than the octavo, called 12mos and 16mos

11. Catechism primers constitute a truly transnational phenomenon and can be found across Europe. See Juska-Bacher et al. (forthcoming)

on how Christian people should live, with mutual respect for each other and the authorities, and not least on how children were to respect and obey their parents. Once children could properly read Luther's *Small Catechism*, they began to learn its parts by heart, one by one. Parallel to this rote-learning, children would continue to train their functional reading skills with the help of a third book: a small book of gospels. This book was printed specifically for children, with small woodcuts marking the beginning of each gospel story. Whereas the ABC was often printed on strong paper for durability, the small catechism and the book of gospels were usually printed on cheap paper in small formats, reducing the cost of these beginners' books.

They would usually be bound, often in very plain bindings of wood or paper, and in most cases they would be the first "proper books" a Nordic child would own.

The fourth book in a child's religious curriculum was a thick exposition to the catechism. In Denmark-Norway, one specific title - Erik Pontoppidan's pietistic *Sandhed til Gudfrygtighed* (1737, translated as *Truth unto Godliness*)[12] - had been mandatory since its publication. During the 1730s, the king had made a Lutheran confirmation compulsory for all young people - with school attendance as a mandatory prerequisite. From then on, all children had to read and then rote-learn Pontoppidan's 769 questions and answers elaborating on the Christian doctrines. At any rate, that was the ideal, and a shortened easy-reader version soon entered the book market.[13]

In some schools a wider selection of religious books, especially Bible stories, was also in use, and sometimes a more varied supply of textbooks was available as well, mainly in urban schools and for private tuition. Almost everywhere, and particularly for boys, corporal punishment was used as an additional "teaching aid" to beat out sinful thoughts and habits.

State, church, and school reforms

The longevity of these teaching patterns and quite similar curricula across the Nordic region can be explained by the important role of Lutheran state churches. Religious minorities were virtually non-existent - with two important exceptions: the Sami religion across the high north of Norway and Sweden-Finland, and the Inuit religion in Greenland.

In the eighteenth century, the Nordic region was divided politically into two conglomerate states: To the west, the Danish king - the head of an absolutist system since 1660 - ruled the kingdoms of Denmark and Norway, the Duchies of Schleswig and Holstein, Iceland, the Faroe Is-

12. The words "translated as" in a parenthesis, following a Scandinavian title, mean that an English translation has been published

13. This small compendium was published by Peder Saxtorph in 1771. It was never officially sanctioned, but was frequently reprinted, just like Pontoppidan's mandatory exposition

lands, Greenland, and minor colonies in the West Indies, India, and Africa. To the east, the Swedish king was in control of Sweden, Finland, and extensive territories along the south-east coast of the Baltic Sea (including modern-day Estonia and Latvia). This political division was reflected in two distinct book markets, with Danish and Swedish, respectively, as the dominant languages for books in the vernacular, including books for children (with ABCs and some other books in Finnish as notable exceptions). Much literature was also imported and read in German, Latin, and French, and well-educated families in Stockholm, Helsinki, Copenhagen, and Bergen would buy some of the same books in German for their children. Quite often these German or French titles would also be translated into Danish and Swedish.

Around the end of the eighteenth century, a number of political and societal changes took place that influenced children's education and the emergence of a special market for children's books. Denmark had experienced a long period of peace and economic prosperity, and Copenhagen in particular was blossoming. This situation changed abruptly with Denmark's involvement in the Napoleonic wars, resulting in military defeats (in 1801 and 1807), the loss of Norway (in 1814), and state bankruptcy (in 1813). Prior to this, major agricultural reforms had been introduced, also stimulated by extensive legislation from the 1780s. The old village communities, where peasants had worked collectively, were broken up, so that each tenant farmer received his own plot of land and thereby became responsible for his own property. These agricultural reforms were soon combined with educational reforms, too.

One of the pioneers in this reform movement was Count Christian Ditlev Reventlow (who played Grandison in Friederike Brun's private stage production). Inspired by Enlightenment thinking in general and German philanthropist thoughts on education and childhood in particular, Reventlow and his like-minded peers wanted to foster the development of more enlightened, self-reliant peasants on their estates - farmers who were good Christians, but who could also read books about new crops and horticulture, write their own letters, and keep their own accounts. A royal committee was set up to prepare national school reforms and, after much delay, five ambitious reforms were issued in 1814, making regular school attendance for seven years mandatory for all Danish boys and girls, with instruction in religion and reading as well as writing and arithmetic. Moreover, teacher-training colleges were introduced to raise the standard of instruction given, with the intention of limiting corporal punishment as part of the legislation.

In most schools the catechism was now supplemented with new readers, such as translations or adaptations of the German philanthropist Friedrich Rochow's *Der Kinderfreund* (1776, "the children's friend").[14] A new period had begun, with school reforms and new ideas of childhood, and with books published explicitly and directly for children as the main target audience.

New perceptions of childhood

School reforms and new books for children were related to a growing interest in childhood among philosophers, educators, and authors. The French philosopher Jean-Jacques Rousseau's *Émile ou de l'Éducation* (1762, translated as *Emile, or On Education*) became a very influential publication across Europe, not because many boys and girls were actually educated like Rousseau's ideal child Émile, but because his radically new perception of childhood kindled a gradual change in the approach to children. In the Nordic countries Rousseau's works were read in French and German - and later in translations as well - but adaptations of his ideas through German philanthropists like Johan Basedow were probably even more

14. The first Danish translation of Rochow was published as *Den danske Børneven* ("the Danish children's friend") in 1777 by J. C. Pingel. Over a period of some 50 years, it appeared in 15 editions on the Danish-Norwegian book market, based on various translations and adaptations (Baden Staffensen 2018)

22

important. Rousseau's idea was that children had natural, inborn qualities that would guide them in their upbringing. The nature of the child, and nature around the child, were considered more valuable in their process of growing up than teachers, books, or schools. On the one hand, Rousseau's interest in education reflects his connection to the Enlightenment; on the other hand, his idealization of the "uncultivated" child growing up in close contact with nature also points towards Romanticism.

These changes in the ideals of childhood, especially among the upper classes, are reflected in the differences in the way Friederike Brun was "presented" as a child in the 1770s, and how she let her own daughter appear around 1800. Her autobiography describes how she had to endure complicated, painful hairstyles complete with small porcelain figurines ("a torture"), and how her body was "held prisoner" by a corset and her feet forced into shoes with very high heels (Brun 1824: 128, 130). In contrast, her daughter Ida (1792-1857) was painted dancing in a garden, wearing flat shoes and a light, loose dress, with her hair hanging "naturally" down her shoulders (see p. 24). A garland of flowers literally entangles the child in nature. She is portrayed as an ideal child, in line with Rousseau's vision: an individual in her own right without adult guidance or control.

The new ideals and perceptions of children were also manifest in the primers and readers of the late eighteenth century, mentioned above. The Danish pastor Thomas Rasmussen (1744-1800) had attacked Luther's catechism as unsuitable and inappropriate for young readers. In his opinion, children needed books made especially for them. In his *ABC* from 1787 (20 pages), Rasmussen went straight from the alphabet to a selection of short stories, each typically taking up just a half or a whole page (7-20 lines). The first was about "The good children at play": Peter, Karen, and Lise. Here, the author pointed

out that playing was more fun after school. Some stories contained warnings (like that of the careless boy Jørgen, who had his leg broken by a horse because he ignored his father's advice about keeping a safe distance), while others pointed to good role models (such as the 5-year-old Lovise, who had been taught to read by her mother and was a better reader than most adults). Another story described a pious girl called Sophia who found comfort in praying to God. Thus, Christian moral was by no means absent, and the specific moral lessons were hardly new. However, the late Enlightenment idea of using children's lives and experiences as a main topic marked a distinctive new phase in children's literature. This trend had begun in Germany, France, and England, and by the 1780s it had also been adapted to the world of Nordic children.[15] Over the following decades, many boys and girls would encounter this alternative sort of children's book at school.[16]

Changes in markets and genres

From the beginning of Friederike's childhood, in the 1770s and 1780s, until the end of Hans Christian's youth around 1820, the number and variety of books explicitly written and published for children increased immensely. During the 1770s, around 100 Danish titles were published for children in Denmark and Norway, averaging 10 a year, whereas this number had quadrupled to around 400 in the 1810s, an average of 40 per year.[17] This growth was linked to improved standards of schooling, to an increased interest in childhood, and, not least, to parents and teachers being prepared to buy such books. A number of individual authors and publishers played essential roles in promoting this development. When *Avis for Børn* (1770–1774, "newspaper for children") appeared, the initiative came from a small group of men who wanted to try their luck as authors, publishers, and entrepreneurs in general.[18] Towards the turn of the century, some people even tried to concentrate their publication activities on this emerging niche in the book market.

One such actor on the new market for children's books was Morten Hallager (1741–1803). Having worked first as a printer and then as a private schoolmaster in Copenhagen, he made a third career for himself as a publisher of children's books. He composed his own very successful primer for early readers in 1791, which appeared in 11 editions. Hallager saw himself as a transnational agent opening the world of European Enlightenment literature to Danish children, and 37 of his 39 titles for children were

15. For more on the general development of the German market for children's books 1750–1800, see Brüggemann & Ewers (1982). On cautionary tales, see Joosen (2006)

16. For more on teaching practices and books used in Copenhagen schools, particularly for girls 1780–1820, see Gold (1996)

17. These numbers are based on a database covering Danish books for children 1750–1849, constructed in connection with ongoing research on children and books; see Appel & Christensen (2017). Comparable data are not available for children's books in Swedish, but the main trends appear to be the same

18. On Danish and Swedish magazines for children in this period, see Christensen (2012) and Svensson (2018), respectively

adaptations from German and French. He stressed that he used the very best international authors and educators, while at the same time "localizing" their writings so they would be relevant to Danish children (Appel, forthcoming). His repertoire included several primers and readers, such as *Godmand eller den danske Børneven* (1798, "Goodman or the Danish children's friend"), based on K. T. Thieme's German original, as well as a number of books on geography and travel accounts for children, including C. C. Dassel's *Den Gutmannske Families Reiser* (1796, "the travels of the Gutmann family"), to which he added a much extended section on Copenhagen. Such books were meant to expand the horizons of child readers, and they included sections on the "new" continents of America and Australia. Several titles focused on scientific topics, including editions of J. C. Bockshammer's *Den astronomiske Børneven* (1796 and 1800, "the astronomical children's friend"). Among his other publications was a Danish translation of French drama for children by M. Berquin, a selection of children's fairytales based on those by the German author C. P. Funke, a handbook on letter-writing for children, and several successful books of language instruction in German and French, composed specifically for Danish children. On the title pages and in the prefaces of his publications, Hallager emphasized that he wanted to entertain *and* educate his young audience. His portfolio of books for children clearly illustrates why, in this period, it would be anachronistic to distinguish sharply between instructional books on the one hand, and "proper" children's books for fun and entertainment on the other. Most books were a combination of the two.[19]

A distinctive feature of many children's books from the 1790s onwards was the increasing use of illustrations. Statements declaring that books contained "colored copperplates" would often be printed on title pages and in newspaper adverts. In the 1800s, at least 8% of book titles

19. Other Danish publishers and printers who prioritized books for children and schools were J. H. Schubothe and A. F. Just. In Sweden, a similar movement towards specialization can be found

for children included such information. In the 1810s, following the above-mentioned crises (and possibly linked to a growing interest in elementary, affordable, and therefore unillustrated schoolbooks), this percentage dropped.[20]

It was also common to borrow books, especially in towns, where commercial lending libraries became popular towards 1800. In some rural districts, pastors and schoolteachers organized small parish libraries, inspired by Enlightenment thinking (Nielsen 1960). Usually, children did not have direct access, but parents and siblings could act as mediators, and the variety of available reading materials thus increased in many households.

Robinson the Younger - **a bestseller**

The idea that reading fiction could be part of an individual's character development was stated in and around texts for both children and adults throughout the eighteenth century. In prefaces to texts for children published in the Nordic region from the 1760s onwards, the intention to cultivate the hearts and minds of young readers was often repeated. The Danish and Norwegian words for this process (*dannelse* / *danning*) and the Swedish word (*bildning*) are both linked to the German term *Bildung*, which is related to "building" and emphasizes a more general formation of the developing individual. Reading was a key instrument in the education of sensitive and enlightened human beings: citizens who could participate constructively in society and thereby strengthen the state.

Rousseau had only recommended one book for Émile: the English author Daniel Defoe's novel *Robinson Crusoe* (1719) - whose main character survives a shipwreck and manages to create his own tiny civilization on a desert island inhabited only by animals and hostile islanders. The progressive German educator Joachim Heinrich Campe (1746-1818) created an adapted version for chil-

20. This estimate is based on the above-mentioned database (see note 17). On technical developments relating to illustrations, see Goldman (2013) and, specifically for children's books, Whalley & Chester (1988)

dren, and soon *Robinson der Jüngere* (1779, translated as *Robinson the Younger*) became a bestseller across Europe – and America. In his preface to the eighth edition, Campe states with pride that the book is used in many schools and has already been translated into all European languages. The first Danish translation, *Robinson den Yngre*, for use in Denmark and Norway, was published in 1784, with a Swedish translation following in 1785.

According to his preface, Campe wanted to entertain children, but also to transmit knowledge, especially about natural history, and to nurture children's virtues and religious sentiments. The representation of vices and virtues in a fictive character was meant to inspire readers to reflect on and improve their own "character building": The child reader "imagines that he himself is Robinson", Campe states (Campe 1814: xvii).[21] As such, he placed dialogues between a fictional father and his family before each chapter to encourage discussions among children and adults. These Socratic dialogues might also be interpreted as basic training in rational thinking, educated conversation, and democratic skills. When Robinson doubts what to do in a specific situation, the father tells his children: "Now, stand up in two parties, and then we shall hear which reasons each of you have for your opinions" (220).

In the Danish translation of Campe's *Robinson der Jüngere*, Robinson's voyage begins and ends in Copenhagen (and not in Hamburg, as Campe's German version does). This was a common way of adapting texts for children to a national context. Since Robinson lands on the shore of a remote island with hardly any tools, much of the plot revolves around his struggle to build a house and provide for his basic needs – water, food, and shelter. One thought-provoking aspect is the way in which child readers are introduced to differences in races and creeds. When Friday, a young native man, appears on the scene, one of the girls, Lotte, says "Fie, what abhorrent human beings,"

21. Here, we refer to the Danish translation from the eighth edition published by Plesner in 1814. For aspects of the Robinson narrative across media, see O'Malley (2012)

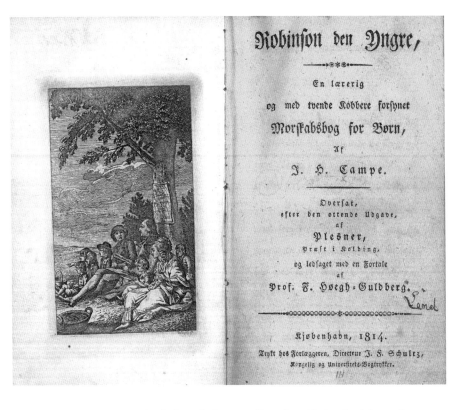

Robinson den Yngre,

En lærerig

og med tvende Kobbere forsynet

Morskabsbog for Børn,

Af

J. H. Campe.

Oversat,
efter den ottende Udgave,
af
Plesner,
Præst i Kolding,
og ledsaget med en Fortale
af
Prof. F. Høegh=Guldberg.

Kjøbenhavn, 1814.

Trykt hos Forlæggeren, Directeur J. S. Schultz,
Kongelig og Universitets-Bogtrykker.

An (ideal) family reading in open space
The frontispiece and title page of *Robinson den Yngre* (1814), a Danish translation of Joachim Campe's *Robinson der Jüngere* (1779, translated as *Robinson the Younger*).
© Royal Danish Library

to which her father replies that if she had been born on the island, she too would have "run about naked, wild, and irrational in the forest" (Campe 1814: 238). His attempt to teach tolerance is clearly mixed with Eurocentric stereotypes of non-Western characters, which is quite typical of children's literature in this period. Later, the children ask their father about slaves, and he explains that it is a despicable practice to deprive other people of their freedom, and one which ought to be fully abandoned (381). Moreover, when, at the beginning of his adventures, Robinson Crusoe finds that the ship taking him from Denmark to England is sinking, seamen from another ship come to the rescue, and one of the boys, Nicolai, asks his father: "I suppose they were Danish?" But his father replies: "Should you help only your compatriots? My dear Nicolai, I do not think you genuinely meant this. If, at this moment, an American were to fall into our little lake, would we then first ask where he came from?!" As it turns out, the compassionate strangers are Turkish (14-15).[22] In this way, Campe and his Danish translator added Enlightenment ideas of humanism and universalism to his children's version of Robinson Crusoe's adventure.

Campe's *Robinson the Younger* - in a number of different versions - became a steady seller on the Nordic book markets throughout the nineteenth century, mainly in translations into the Nordic languages, but also in adapted German editions used for language teaching. However, while the supply of children's books around 1820 was much larger and more varied than half a century before, specific children's books like Campe's novel were still primarily available to privileged children in major cities. Throughout this period, the majority of Nordic children encountered few books, if any, beyond the limited curriculum presented to them at school.

22. In the German text, the boy asks his father whether the sailors were from Hamburg, and the father replies that the saviors were "keine Hamburger, keine Europäer, keine Kristen, sondern – **Türken** (...)" ("not from Hamburg, nor from Europe, nor Christians, but **Turks**" (Campe 1819: 34). Bold used as in the original

Chapter 3.

The child as a future patriotic citizen, 1820–1900

Most Nordic children growing up in the nineteenth century had access to an increasing amount of media and genres produced for, and targeting, a child audience. Technical innovations in book production and greater attentiveness to children's needs contributed to expanding and differentiating the market. Children's poetry and fairytales became widespread genres, much inspired by Romantic ideals of children's "natural" imagination. Raising the child to become a member of the nation state was a strong ambition reflected in many readers, history books, and songbooks made for use in schools and private homes. Children's magazines became widely read, and the picturebook for children emerged as a new medium.

Anton and Ida

The autobiography of the Danish teacher and author Anton Nielsen (1827–1897), who grew up in a poor rural setting, and letters from Ida Holten Thiele (1830-1862), who had a privileged childhood in Copenhagen, offer insights into the variety of media ensembles encountered by different children. These two examples help to illustrate that there was no such thing as a "typical" nineteenth-century child. They point to the importance of children's own initiatives and interaction with adults, and they also remind us how old genres and literary traditions often met new texts and trends when children composed their own media repertoires.

Anton Nielsen was born as the son of a poor school-teacher in a village about 75 kilometers from Copenhagen. In his autobiography, he describes how books were scarce in his childhood home (Nielsen 1894). However, oral literary culture played an important part, and narratives, songs, and drama were performed in the old, dilapidated house – the accommodation that was part of his father's salary as a teacher:

"In our house we loved the twilight hour, when we would sit by Mother around the stove and watch the fire. She would be knitting stockings. It was her only rest during the day, and she enjoyed it immensely. We were never told ghost stories, but Mother knew several old fairytales, which we children wanted to hear over and over again, even though we knew them by heart." (Nielsen 1894: 112)

Anton's mother taught him to read using an illustrated ABC published by Morten Hallager, and years later the author recalled the thick, heavy-duty paper and the poorly done illustrations. At school they had to rote-learn the complicated religious sentences written by Bishop Balle in his rationalist exposition to the catechism (which, since the 1790s, had substituted the pietistic exposition by Bishop Pontoppidan, mentioned earlier). They did this without pleasure. In contrast, a songbook for adults was the first book Anton ever owned personally: "I lived in the songbook from morning till evening," he states (Nielsen 1894: 88). He also proudly describes how he was able to gain access to reading material by working as a sort of book detective at neighboring farms. Once he had found out where the farmers normally kept their chapbooks – small books with entertaining stories, including the one about Anton's favorite character, the carnivalesque figure of *Till Uglspil* or *Eulenspiegel* – he would politely ask to see the books, then to borrow them. Another welcome help for this self-proclaimed "devourer of novels" came from a pastor's daughter, who had noticed his interest in books and allowed him to borrow several contemporary popular novels for adults, which she had received through a reading society. The author also describes how he and other children would entertain and inform each other by telling stories, singing together, and doing small performances. Thanks to these interactions with adults and peers, and not least thanks to his own initiative, the boy managed to compose a varied media repertoire, despite initial practical and financial obstacles. Later in life he became a teacher, held a position at one of the new Danish folk high schools (see p. 38), and became one of the country's most popular authors of realistic fiction in the second half of the nineteenth century.

The contrast between Anton Nielsen's situation, and his access to media, culture, and entertainment, and that of Ida Holten Thiele is striking. On his rare visits to Copenhagen, Anton may have crossed the prominent square of Kongens Nytorv, where he could have admired the Royal Theatre and perhaps seen a young Hans Christian Andersen pass through the gates to the Royal Academy of Fine Arts at Charlottenborg. Andersen was a friend of Ida's father, Just Mathias Thiele (1795-1874), who was a professor at the academy and lived in one of the large apartments facing the square. In an exquisite book Thiele made for his baby daughter Ida, who was born in 1830, he reported the details of the early years of a childhood surrounded by luxury and love. When Ida's mother died in 1835, the five-year-old girl and her sister went to live with their grandparents, and from her letters to her father we know quite a lot about her upbringing and (home) schooling. Ida had a private female tutor, who taught her to read and write. She learned about religion, geography, and history, and also had a "Mr. Valentin", who taught her French. When she visited her father in Copenhagen, the dance lessons she received at home were supplemented with instruction by August Bournonville, the famous ballet master of the Royal Theatre.

While Anton Nielsen writes that his family could not afford to send letters because paper and stamps were too expensive, Ida was encouraged to practice the art of letter-writing. She thus came to master an important genre for an educated and privileged girl, and enabled her father to follow her everyday life, the improvements in her reading and writing skills, and the development of her character. Ida wrote in her letters about what she read, and reported on the performances and plays she was involved in, her social circles, and the balls and theater plays she attended. Ida Holten Thiele was, in fact, the girl to whom Hans Christian Andersen told his fairytale "Den lille Idas blomster" (1835, translated as "Little Ida's Flowers"), but even though the production of children's books was increasing, printed books seem relatively absent in Ida's letters, most likely because their presence was evident. Instead, she stresses her favorite genre, drama, when mentioning her model theater, the plays she performed with her cousins, and the professional plays she attended. Nevertheless, the life choices Ida had as a young woman were quite limited: The aim of her education was to marry well, which she did. She had three children and died at the age of 32.

Nation-building and modernization

Several important cultural and societal changes took place in Denmark and the rest of the Nordic region during the decades when Ida and Anton – and their children – were growing up. These changes influenced the contexts and conditions of book production, media consumption, and education, as well as the contents of literature for children and young people.

Many new developments had to do with nation-building. In the nineteenth century, borders were changing. A number of wars were fought, and new definitions of national identity and nationhood developed. In 1814, near the end of the Napoleonic wars, Denmark had lost Norway, which adopted its own constitution before becoming a (largely independent) part of Sweden until 1905. Around 1850, Denmark sold its small Asian and African colonies (it kept the three Virgin Islands in the Caribbean until 1917). Even more important were the two Danish–Prussian wars over sovereignty in the duchies of Schleswig and Holstein in 1848-1850 and 1864, respectively. In the latter, Denmark suffered a devastating defeat, and both duchies, including what is today the southern part of Jutland (Sønderjylland), came under Prussian rule. Patriotic movements and anti-German sentiments grew before and especially after the defeat of 1864. Denmark was no longer a large conglomerate state, but a small nation state with its North Atlantic dependencies and a single colony. New ideas were being cultivated about the unique character of the Danish mother tongue (modersmålet), the history of the fatherland (fædrelandet), and the Danish people (folket), and they were clearly evident in politics, education, and texts and media produced for and used by children.

These developments were in no way an exclusively Danish phenomenon, but ran parallel to similar movements and sentiments in other European and Nordic countries. In Norway, the country's independence from Denmark had led to an increased focus on what was specific to the new nation, and from the mid-nineteenth century many efforts were put into creating a written Norwegian language that could be differentiated from Danish. Gradually, the Danish and Norwegian book markets, which until then had been one market, began to separate. The first children's book explicitly aimed at Norwegian children was Maurits Hansen's *Godmand eller den norske Børneven* (1834, "Goodman or the Norwegian children's friend"). In 1888, the steady-selling picturebook *Norsk Billedbog for Børn* ("Norwegian picturebook for children") was published with the explicit aim of presenting Norwegian popular poetry and images of Norwegian landscapes to children.[23]

Sweden also underwent major changes. It lost Finland in 1809, but instead Norway came under Swedish rule from 1814. In Finland, the population were no longer subjects of the Swedish king but of the Russian emperor. The nineteenth century in Finland was a period of social hardship, but also of a strong national awakening that celebrated Finnish language and literature. From around 1850, a Scandinavian or Nordic movement appeared as well, often in tandem with the region's national movements. The movement's supporters, including many academics and teachers, advocated *Scandinavian* history and cultural heritage and focused on a common and more democratic past (during the Viking and Middle Ages) shared by Scandinavian brothers and sisters, in contrast to a conservative, militaristic Germany. The Gothic typeface, which had been standard in Nordic books for centuries and was even called "Danish letters", increasingly came to be associated with German culture. From 1871 (following Denmark's defeat in 1864), children in Danish schools were to be taught to read and write primarily Latin letters, in contrast to what after 1864 came to be termed "German

23. Until around 1820, most books for Norwegian children – with Danish as the written language – had been produced in Copenhagen. Traditionally, Willum Stephansen's *Lommebog for Børn* (1796, "pocketbook for children") is considered the first Norwegian children's book, as it was printed in Trondheim

letters", aligning Denmark with her Scandinavian brothers and sisters. In Sweden, the changeover to Latin letters had occurred earlier, due to influence from France.

Another strong driver of societal and cultural change across the Nordic countries was population growth, combined with (relatively late) industrialization, urbanization, emigration, and the rise of a new working class. Until the early nineteenth century, the social and economic structures of Scandinavian countries had remained relatively stable, though the populations had been growing since the 1760s. Denmark went from some 770,000 people around 1770 to roughly 1.2 million around 1820.[24] Until 1820 or so, about 80% of the Danish population lived in rural districts, and in most other parts of the Nordic region the figure was nearly 90%. However, new methods of industrial production were being introduced, and the effects of the eighteenth-century agricultural reforms became more visible. What is more, the old social order was breaking up, resulting in greater geographical and social mobility. Further population growth and industrialization contributed to yet more urbanization and the emergence of a new class of industrial workers and groups of urban poor living in slums. The capitals of Copenhagen and Stockholm quadrupled their populations during this period, and major cities like Aarhus and Gothenburg developed rapidly. Many more Nordic children than before grew up in towns and cities – and experienced moving from the countryside to an urban environment. Some children also belonged to families that emigrated to the United States and Canada, which conversely meant that other children had to bid friends and relatives farewell.

The nineteenth century was also a period of profound political change. In Denmark, the system of absolute monarchy came under increasing pressure from political and religious movements in the 1830s and 1840s, and the Danish king was forced to adopt a new constitu-

24. Danish figures according to https://danmarkshistorien.dk/leksikon-og-kilder/vis/materiale/danmarks-befolkningsudvikling/. In comparison, the Swedish population reached approximately 2.6 million in 1820

tion in 1849, a development provoked in part by the first Schleswig war. Absolutism was abolished, and restricted democracy was introduced. Only 15% of the population (financially independent men) had voting rights, but freedom of speech and freedom of religion were among the new rights guaranteed by the Danish Constitution of 1849.[25] However, democracy remained a contested phenomenon in all countries. The political changes across the Nordic region were accompanied by the liberalization of trade and commerce in the second half of the nineteenth century.

Ideals and realities surrounding children

Wars, nationalism, and political changes came to influence the lives and literature of children. In Denmark, following the adoption of the new constitution in 1849, compulsory schooling was changed into mandatory teaching (1855), which secured parents the right to choose freely how to instruct their children. At a time when democracy was commonly subject to skepticism, education was seen as a key instrument to legitimize and strengthen it. The phenomenon of *højskoler* ("folk high schools", which still exist today) proved successful. These were a new type of boarding school for young men and women from rural areas, meant to widen their horizons and enable them to "learn for life", rather than educating them to pass certain exams. Similar ideals about how to teach children, often combined with protests against rote-learning and bookishness, influenced numerous new, independent, and privately run elementary schools often related to the religious and national awakening inspired by the influential theologian and author N. F. S. Grundtvig (1783-1872).[26] In the latter half of the nineteenth century, private and public libraries, and reading clubs and societies – like the one Anton Nielsen managed to access indirectly – were

25. Norway had had a democratic constitution since 1814, and Sweden moved in a democratic direction with a bicameral parliamentary system that was introduced in 1866. See Gustafsson (2017: 173-181)

26. For Grundtvig's thoughts on childhood, see Bunge (2017)

founded in many local communities, also inspired by the increasing political mobilization in society.

At the same time, there was a tendency towards more detailed regulation of children's schooling. Danish and history became important school subjects, meant to strengthen children's love of their mother tongue and their fatherland, especially following the country's defeat in 1864. Privately run elementary schools had been predominant, but this began to change, especially in the cities, due to rapid population growth and the hard living conditions of children in the slums. Large municipal schools took the lead, representing a new approach to children, with professional, specialized teachers, including many female teachers, and assisted by scientific experts in child medicine and pedagogy. Hygiene gained awareness, and a new interest arose in the study of infants and toddlers, leading to the first experimental nurseries and kindergartens. More attention was also paid to children's access to books through libraries, albeit with huge geographical differences. From the 1850s onwards, all schools in Copenhagen had set up school libraries, and several provincial towns followed suit. One school library, in Sønderborg, included 533 volumes in 1861. In the countryside, however, financing was often lacking, and children might be asked to pay a small fee each month to borrow books (Kastberg 1967).

These cultural and societal changes would often manifest themselves directly in the content of books for children – and in children's lives more generally. For example, the phenomenon of war was present in the childhood toys of the influential literary scholar Georg Brandes (1842-1927). As he explains in his autobiography: "The fact that a war was going on created a whole new interest in tin soldiers. One could not get too many boxes of them. They were placed in battalions and companies: They excelled in attacks, they stormed, were wounded and fell" (Brandes 1905: 24). Tin soldiers were main characters in stories such as Hans Christian Andersen's "Den standhaftige Tin-soldat" (1838, translated as "The Steadfast Tin Soldier"). On broadsheets – inexpensive printed sheets available at markets – soldiers, kings, and battle scenes were frequent motifs.[27]

The strong interest in Danish history became visible in children's schoolbooks. In 1777, Ove Malling had written a book about true patriotic deeds performed by men from Denmark, Norway, and Holstein, but the emphasis now changed. From the 1820s onwards, such books mainly described Danish events and heroes, as in adaptations of E. C. F. Munthe's books on the geography and history of "the Fatherland" and in Peder Hjort's popular reader *Den danske Børneven* (1839, "the Danish children's friend"). Following the defeat of 1864, this tendency became even more pronounced, for example in N. B. Rom's *Fædrelands-historie* (1875, "history of the fatherland"), published in 49 editions over the following 30 years and accompanied by evocative pictures arranged on a type of explanatory wall chart called *anskuelsestavler*. Inspired especially by the novels of Sir Walter Scott, historical novels by the Danish author B. S. Ingemann (1789-1862) became popular reading across generations, highlighting episodes from medieval Denmark, and including such titles as *Erik Menveds Barndom* (1828, "the childhood of [king] Eric Menved").

The shifts in Danish political culture and society can also be traced in contemporary children's books, for instance in Caën's children's drama *Prøven paa Slaget ved Fredericia* (1850, "rehearsal for the battle at Fredericia"), published to be performed by children in private homes. The plot features child characters who must make a difficult decision, objecting to the instructions of the fictitious adults prior to their drama performance, and a vote has to be cast. Even the girls are encouraged to participate in the discussions and in reaching the final decision!

27. On the rich German print culture, also for children, including broadsheets, see Vogel (1981). For Denmark, see Stybe (1983)

The rapidly changing social environment of industrial cities was not a central theme as such in children's books, but it was nonetheless present, often in descriptions of orphans and poor children suffering hardship. Most often they would be helped by kind-hearted middle-class children, as in Johan Krohn's popular classic poem *Peters Jul* (1866, "Peter's Christmas"), but sometimes they would not, as in Hans Christian Andersen's "Den lille Pige med Svovlstikkerne" (1846, translated as "The Little Match Girl"), in which the main character dies on a cold winter's night. More detailed fiction about urban misery was also available for all age groups in translated literature from England, including the famous Charles Dickens novel *Oliver Twist* (first translated into Danish in 1840).

Romantic ideas, fairytales, and poetry

During the nineteenth century, authors and philosophers across Europe linked children and childhood to fantasy, fairytales, and literature as an aesthetic mode of expression; this was a strong trend in the Nordic countries, too. When the most popular and influential contemporary Danish poet, Adam Oehlenschläger (1779–1850), published his translation of some of the fairytales of the Brothers Grimm in 1816, he included "children's fairytales" and added the following explanation: "Normally, children have a more powerful imagination than adults. Just as they must learn experience and reason from us, from them we ought to learn to preserve imagination and innocence" (Oehlenschläger 1816, vol. 2: xxxiii). These sentences reflect what could be called a new ideology of childhood, which advanced a more natural, simple, and innocent state of being that was connected to imagination and fantastical thinking, and thereby also to poetry and artistic creation.

Oehlenschläger's inclusion of fairytales for children and his description of the child's imagination were related to the German philosopher Friedrich Schiller's idea of the relationship between children's play and aesthetic creation in *Über die ästhetische Erziehung des Menschen* (1795, translated as *On the Aesthetic Education of Man*), and to the Brothers Grimm's publication of German *Volks- und Hausmärchen* (1812-1815, translated as *German Popular Tales and Household Stories*). Songs and stories told by "the people" were collected, transcribed, and put into print. It was J. M. Thiele - the real "little Ida's" father – who first followed in the footsteps of the Brothers Grimm on Danish soil and published the stories he had collected among peasants on Zealand as *Danske Folkesagn* (1818-1823, "Danish folk tales"). In Norway, Jørgen Moe and P. C. Asbjørnsen collected and published *Norske Folke- og Børneeventyr* (1841-1844, "Norwegian folk and children's tales"). The collection *Svenska Folksagor och Äfventyr* (1844-1849, "Swedish folk and fairytales") by Gunnar Olof Hultén-Cavallius and George Stephens also appeared around this time.

Should texts for children appeal to their imagination, or were realistic narratives combining education and entertainment preferable? Around 1800, answers to this question were linked to changing ideas about the role of the author and of literature. Across Europe, authors who had their debuts around the turn of the nineteenth century opposed the Enlightenment idea that reading literature ought to be part of the moral education of readers, for instance through exemplary characters. Authors linked to or inspired by Romantic movements perceived the artist as having a special sort of sensibility and sense of beauty, related to nature and the divine. They held that divine inspiration, not reason and knowledge, ought to be the point of departure for creating literature; this established a link between the artist and the child, as both had privileged access to the power of the imagination.

A Danish example of the discrepancy between old and new ways of thinking is reflected in the Hans Christian

Andersen fairytale "Little Ida's Flowers" from 1835, mentioned earlier. This story is set in a living room, where the character Ida asks a visiting student why her flowers look so dead. The student engages in a lively conversation with the child, explaining that the flowers are tired because they have attended a ball at the King's castle. A grumpy old councilor sitting in a corner comments: "How can anyone stuff a child's head with such nonsense – such stupid fantasy?" (Andersen [1835]: n.p.).[28] In a dreamlike sequence, a doll dressed up as the councilor ends up being ridiculed and beaten by other characters. A rather critical reviewer of the first collection of fairytales by Andersen stated that "Little Ida's Flowers" was the "least feeble" piece in the volume, but he was still disappointed that "this fairytale did not contain a moral either" (Nielsen 1986: 125). This remark was quite typical of debates concerning children's literature in the mid-nineteenth century.

28. Translation by Jean Hersholt

Poems and picturebooks

In continuation of the idea of a kinship between childhood and imagination, poems became a favorite genre in publications for children from the 1830s onwards. One of the reasons why poems enjoyed such popularity was that they could be set to music and sung. Following the Danish school acts of 1814, lessons in singing became part of the mandatory curriculum for urban schools, and children in the countryside were to learn how to sing too. Subsequently, various anthologies of songs were published, including Frederik Barfod's *Poetisk Læsebog for Børn og Barnlige Sjæle* (1835-1836, "poetic reader for children and childish spirits") – explicitly "for use at school and in the home." The latter suggests a reading culture that transcended the boundaries between home and school and between child and adult, known from previous centuries. According to Barfod's preface, one of the aims of his collection was to make children acquainted with beauty.

Young children were also addressed as individuals with an ability to appreciate poetry. In 1837, B. S. Ingemann published *Morgensange for Børn* ("morning songs for children"), consisting of seven songs set to music by the popular composer C. E. F. Weyse. These songs were written to be used in one of Denmark's very first public institutions for children under the age of five, established in 1835.[29] Some of the songs are narrated by children themselves, a "we" of poor children whose parents must work, but who find a home not only at the institution, but also in the arms of Jesus, who is depicted as a close friend of children. Another song, *Lysets Engel*, metaphorically describes the sunrise as an "angel of light," who moves from sky to earth to kiss the child lying in the cradle. Some of the songs were soon included in songbooks meant for use in schools, and along with several texts by Adam Oehlenschläger and N. F. S. Grundtvig they were set to music by contemporary composers and are still sung in the twenty-first century. Most of these poems are either religious or strongly national or both, as they deal with Christian content, Nordic mythology, Danish history, the beauty of the Danish landscape, or brave men from Denmark's past.

In Barfod's collection, the new idea of poetry written explicitly for an audience of children was reflected in the inclusion of fables by the German author Johan Wilhelm Hey (1789-1854), translated by the upcoming Danish poet Christian Winther (1796-1876). Hey's fables had been published in Germany in 1833 and owed much of their reputation to the accompanying illustrations, which were by Otto Speckter. Thus, a second reason for the popularity of poetry was the emerging picturebook industry in the Nordic countries, in which the typical layout consisted of a poem placed underneath an illustration on each page, often in a large quarto format. Painters who were also involved in the contemporary promotion of a special "Danish" landscape made the illustrations. Early examples of

29. For English translations of the songs, see Krabbe (1996: 83-90)

such books are H. V. Kaalund and J. Th. Lundbye's *Fabler for Børn* (1845, "fables for children") and Christian Winther and Martinus Rørbye's *Fem og tyve Billeder for smaa Børn* (1846, "twenty-five pictures for small children"). In the latter, the first illustration and the accompanying text read like a manual for picturebook-reading. The text explains that the mother will gather her children close around her, and that everything she reads will also be represented in pictures. Finally, the text encourages readers that "If you also want to get to know the book / you just need to turn the page" (Winther 1846, n.p.). A picturebook was a new and rare medium in many families, as this introduction on its proper use indicates. The involvement of well-established painters and poets in the production of picturebooks reflects the idea of children as individuals who are open to aesthetic modes of expression. As mentioned before, the production of picturebooks in Norway was part of a wish to promote a specific Norwegian literature, culture, and landscape, and the same was the case in Sweden, where *Svenska barnboken* ("the Swedish children's book") was published in 1886 (Westin 2004).

Publishers and new media

Major technological changes took place in book production during the nineteenth century. Paper had traditionally been made out of old rags in paper mills, but beginning in the 1810s it was also produced industrially using wood pulp, at much lower costs, and this method became the dominant one from the 1820s onwards. The classic printing press, operated by two skilled craftsmen, was substituted with the so-called rotary press (in Denmark from the 1850s), which used continuous rolls of paper rather than single sheets. This resulted in a much faster, more efficient, and cheaper printing process. Another major innovation was lithography, a technology involving the application of oil, fat, or wax to the surface of a lithographic limestone. This enabled the mass production of high-quality pictures at a reasonable price. And whereas, traditionally, all coloration (of woodcuts and copper plates) had been added manually, in the 1870s it became possible to add colors as part of the industrial process (Goldman 2013: 238-242). This helped to make fully illustrated picturebooks more widely accessible. In general, children's books became cheaper, thanks to the new production methods, but at the same time the market for children's books became more differentiated, with beautifully bound and richly illustrated books available next to modest pamphlets printed on cheap paper – and even single-sheet publications like broadsheets. The first examples of children's books with pop-up features and toy elements appeared in Denmark during this period.[30]

30. An example is *Isabelles Forvand-linger eller Pigen i sex Skikkelser. En underholdende Billedbog for Piger med syv kolorerede bevægelige Kobbere* (1823, "the transfor-mations of Isabella, or the girl in six figures: an enter-taining picture-book for girls with seven illuminated movable copper-plates"). It was adopted by H. F. Popp from similar publications by S. J. Fuller in London. On the materiality of such books, see Field (2019)

One of the most remarkable agents on the Danish book market to make use of these technologies in his pro-duction of children's books was Christian Steen of Copen-hagen. Steen was also a producer of paper and maps, but children's books became the heart of his business and re-mained so for more than five decades. Several of his books from the 1830s stood out because of their high-quality illustrations and their unusual physical formats, which were well suited for illustrations. In contrast to traditional octavos in an upright position, several of Steen's titles were printed in a more squarish or even elongated format. Until around 1840, virtually all books had been distributed in raw materials, meaning in piles of printed paper sheets that were sent to local booksellers and bookbinders. This allowed customers to make their own decisions about the binding – or even to make a cheap binding themselves. From the 1840s onwards, Steen introduced the latest Eu-ropean fashion, publishing a number of children's books in attractive white, yellow, or green bindings straight from his printing house. Other Danish publishers adopted sim-ilar methods in competition with Steen, and in Sweden, too, publishing houses such as the Gleerup and Bonnier family-owned companies in Lund and Stockholm, respec-tively, invested in books for children and schools.

Children's books had been advertised in newspapers since the late eighteenth century, but Steen and many of his contemporaries extended their marketing of children's books, not least as the ideal Christmas present. The de-mand for children's reading materials was so great that printing factories in the German town of Neuruppin pro-duced series of broadsheets and games for children with

Robinsons Reise og Eventyr.
(Et nyt underholdende Terning-Spil.)

Robinson as a
board game
"Robinson's Travels
and Adventures",
printed as a
broadsheet in
Neuruppin,
Germany, for a
Danish audience
c. 1850. © Royal
Danish Library

Danish texts, exclusively for the Danish market. Colorful pictures were produced not only for private consumption, but also for educational purposes. From the 1880s onwards, visually powerful wall charts were produced for schools in huge numbers, supplementing sparsely illustrated schoolbooks on history, geography, natural history, and religion. Many mechanical inventions and scientific discoveries of the nineteenth century were explained to children via wall charts, and they were a key source for many children imagining people, animals, and plants in other parts of the world.[31]

31. The largest European collection of such educational wall charts can be found in Denmark, at Aarhus University. Images can be accessed at https://skolehistorie.au.dk/en/collections/the-collection-of-wallcharts/

An increasingly popular medium in all of the Nordic countries was children's magazines. As in the eighteenth century, these consisted of a mixture of informative texts and fiction, riddles, prose, and poetry, and gradually illustrations became an integrated part of the format. In the latter half of the century, children would encounter new trends and texts, including the first printed versions of Hans Christian Andersen's stories, not as separate books, but as articles or chapters in cheap magazines. Many children's magazines were written and published by schoolteachers who wanted to provide large groups of children with appropriate and affordable reading materials. Many materials, texts and pictures alike, were imported from English and American magazines, often with very limited adaptation, making these magazines a truly transnational genre (Kaasa 2019). In some cases the same stories traveled from Scandinavia to America and back again, as in the case of the Norwegian fairytale about "Lille Alvilde" (1829, translated as "Little Alvilde").[32] Across the Nordic countries, various religious communities and charitable organizations, for instance societies for the protection of animals, would publish their own children's monthly or bimonthly magazine. These were supplemented by popular Christmas magazines, such as the Swedish *Jultomten* (1891-1934, "father christmas"), which was remarkable for its continuous publication throughout more than four decades, and for being printed in 200,000 copies around 1893 (Svensson 2018: 140).

Some popular children's magazines were published and read across Nordic borders, a practice also assisted by the above-mentioned pan-Scandinavian and Nordic movements. The Finnish-Swedish author and publisher Zacharias Topelius (1818-1898) was involved in the publication of *Eos* (1854-1866), printed in Åbo in the Swedish-speaking part of Finland, and later in that of *Läsning för barn* ("reading for children"), published by Bonnier in Stockholm from

32. Originally by Maurits Hansen (1829). See Bjørkøy & Kaasa (forthcoming)

1865 to 1896. Topelius was a central figure in Swedish-Finnish Romantic literature and the Finnish national movement, and he wrote numerous texts for children's magazines. His short stories were reprinted in book formats and translated into all Nordic languages, and they were still available on the market in the twentieth century. *Barnens Julrosor | Børnenes Juleroser* (1884-1929, "the children's christmas roses") was partly a Nordic co-production with contributions from some of the region's finest illustrators.

In Sweden, Stina Quint (1859-1924) became one of the most successful publishers of children's magazines. Educated as a teacher, she was the founder and director of the successful and long-lived *Folkskolans Barntidning* (1892-1949, "the children's journal of the public school") (Svensson 2018: 140). In the latter half of the nineteenth century, teacher-training colleges especially for women had been established, and it became increasingly possible for women to support themselves by teaching, in some cases combining this with an income from writing, translating, and publishing children's fiction. Short stories and novels written by women began to appear across Denmark, Norway, and Sweden from the 1830s onwards, and they began to feature girls as main characters more often.[33]

During the decades from 1820 to 1900 the market for children's books had developed and expanded. While many children would still access and combine traditional genres and media, including crossover fiction, larger numbers of more varied books written and produced specifically for children had become available – from exclusive picturebooks to inexpensive schoolbooks and children's magazines.

33. Andersson (2021) provides analyses of girl characters, citizenship, and girls' books in Sweden in 1832-1921, and Birkeland et al. (2018) write quite extensively on Norwegian female authors, while Øster (2002) is a rare example of scholarly attention to Danish female authors of children's literature in the nineteenth century

Chapter 4.

The child
as a fellow citizen,
1900–1950

During the first half of the twentieth century, the Nordic welfare states came into being. Attention to children and their needs was reflected in more public libraries than before with children's departments, which also played a part in the expanding children's book market. Children gained access to new media such as radio and films, and novels for children – including series directed specifically at boys or girls – came to be widely read. Several Nordic authors and illustrators enjoyed popularity in neighboring countries, and some gained international renown and made a long-lasting impact, not least the Swedish author Astrid Lindgren (1907–2002). Progressive educators, authors, and illustrators addressed children as creative fellow citizens in a modern society.

Tove and Jens Otto

In their autobiographies, Jens Otto Krag (1914–1978) and Tove Ditlevsen (1917–1976) dedicate space to describing their interest in books and other media, as well as teachers who – for better or for worse – were influential in their lives. Krag grew up in a relatively poor family in the provincial town of Randers, 400 kilometers from the Danish capital of Copenhagen. He went on to become an important person in the development of the Danish welfare state, serving as prime minister in governments led by the Social Democrats in 1962–1968 and 1971–1972. Ditlevsen grew up in a small two-room apartment in Vesterbro, a part of Copenhagen mainly populated by working-class families like her own, before she became a widely read author of both adult and children's literature.[34]

In her autobiography, Tove Ditlevsen refers to her first day of school at Enghavevejens Skole as a "revelation and inner shock," and a defining event for her entire career as an author (Ditlevsen 1975: 11). What so overwhelmed her was the confrontation with a genre and a mode of expression that was completely new to her. The female teacher of her class handed out hymn books and explained that every day they would sing a hymn, but the teacher's voice sounded alone when she started singing the Romantic poet B. S. Ingemann's hymn "Gud ske tak og lov" ("God be praised this day") (see p. 44). Tove writes about her reaction: "The beautiful and simple words, the rhyme and the melody enchanted and moved me so intensely that I burst into tears" (Ditlevsen 1975: 12). The other children laughed at her, but the compassionate female teacher put her hands on Tove's shoulders and asked her kindly if she hadn't ever heard a hymn before? The answer was no. In Tove's atheist home the canon consisted of workers' songs, not hymns. The school and this specific teacher opened her eyes to new kinds of texts, and before long Tove knew the hymns by heart. She smuggled the "wonderful hymnbook" into the only place where she could be alone: the small toilet that had recently been installed in the family's apartment. Her father had also provided her with reading material even before she began attending school. For her

34. Ditlevsen's three autobiographical works have recently been published in English by Penguin as *The Copenhagen Trilogy* (2019) and in German by Aufbau as *Der Kopenhagen-Trilogie* (2021)

fifth birthday, he gave his daughter a copy of the fairytales of the Brothers Grimm, bought in an antiquarian bookshop.

Like readers in previous centuries, Tove was taught to read and write by her mother. Allegedly, her mother was bored by reading aloud, so "she found it very sensible to help me manage on my own" (Ditlevsen 1975: 9). In her autobiographical text from the 1970s, the mature writer recalls how word games were the only sort of game she wanted to play. While she had found her own school-reader inspiring, not least for its inclusion of medieval ballads, she was not interested in contemporary children's literature about "spoiled upper-class children, who in order to endure their tedious lives got themselves involved in artificial conflicts with their well-meaning parents and were sent to expensive boarding schools" (77). At the age of 10 she began to write poems in a notebook, and the last of these poems, written when Ditlevsen was 15, was included in her first collection of poetry, *Pigesind* (1939, "a girl's mind"). In sum, Tove read a variety of genres, both texts originally written in Danish and translated texts, and she preferred older poetry directed at a mixed audience to contemporary fiction published for children.

Meanwhile, in the first or second grade, Jens Otto also wrote a poem that he still remembered decades later: "Da Jesus op af graven stod / han spiste på en gulerod" ("When Jesus rose up from his grave / he ate a carrot by the cave") (Krag 1969: 8). The lines were written in the margins of his hymnbook. According to Krag's autobiography, he was inspired by religious poetry, and he "simply combined what I learned in school with the familiar stuff of daily life, and I was also a bit proud of the rhyme" (8). A classmate showed the poem to their strict female teacher, who sent Jens Otto home from school with a note for his mother. Mrs. Krag did not make a big deal out of the episode and threw the letter away, but the next day

Jens Otto was once again called to the desk of the "offi-cious educator" for further "inquisitorial" questioning (11). These events are described in detail and convey the au-thor's recollection of a child's intense feeling of frustration at his teacher's misuse of power and inability to see the production of the poem for what it was from the child's point of view.

In spite of his curiosity about and general joy in read-ing, Jens Otto was bored at school and felt he was "wasting time under the capriciousness of foreign wills" (Krag 1969: 11). Besides books, the boy was interested in new media, and since his father had tried to set up a business produc-ing and selling radios, his family got one too, so that they could listen to sermons, light opera, comedies, and polit-ical speeches – including some by Hitler and some by the Danish politician and social reformer K. K. Steincke. After the radio business failed, his father ran a small cigar shop, where Jens Otto attended to the customers after school – when he was not reading popular novels for adults by Jules Verne and the Danish author Henrik Pontoppidan, who had received the 1917 Nobel Prize in literature. Another of Jens Otto's preferred activities was going to the cinema with his father on Sundays to watch Hollywood movies, including comedies with Buster Keaton and Charlie Chap-lin. After they returned, Jens Otto would recount the plots to his mother. On the day he graduated from high school, Jens Otto Krag went down to the port in Randers, spent a cold night as a steerage passenger on a steamboat, and ar-rived in Copenhagen the next morning, ready to study at the university there and begin moving upwards in society.

Implicitly, both authors create a narrative in which poor children depend on adult support, but perhaps even more so on their own will and determination when it came to influencing their access to books. Another noteworthy fact is that they both remember their hymnbooks and their readers, which points to a strong continuity in the range of books available to children across centuries. In Krag's account, the important role of new electronic media in children's lives is also worth noting.

Childhood and the emerging welfare state

At the turn of the century, books by two prominent Swedish authors reflect a greater awareness of children and their literature. In *Barnets århundreda* (1900, translated as *The Century of the Child*), the Swedish author, teacher, and educationalist Ellen Key addressed children's well-being in the family, and in society as a whole, from a social-Darwinist point of view. The Nobel Prize-winning author Selma Lagerlöf published *Nils Holgerssons underbara resa genom Sverige* (1906-1907, translated as *The Wonderful Adventures of Nils*), which described Swedish topography, nature, and culture to Swedish schoolchildren, as experienced by the boy Nils, who flies across the country on a white goose. This book can be seen as the predecessor to books appearing later in the twentieth century that promoted active, adventurous children who could travel on their own (see p. 63-64).

Around 1900, Nordic children were growing up in societies in which democracy as a phenomenon was still under development. In Denmark, political parties had gradually emerged in the latter half of the nineteenth century, and in 1901, after decades of conflicts, the so-called parliamentary system was formally recognized. From this point on, the king would always have to appoint a government in accordance with the majority of the *Folketing*, the first chamber of parliament. Across the Nordic countries women were increasingly raising their voices to obtain democratic rights, inspired by the international Suffragette movement. Danish women gained the right to vote at local elections in 1908, and in 1915 a revised constitution was approved by a general referendum, giving full democratic rights to women along with some other previously excluded groups, such as adults without an independent household.[35] During this period, national and local newspapers became widely read, and the newspapers in many children's homes would represent a clear political affiliation to one of the main political parties.

Another major change at the turn of the century was the regulation of industrial affairs and the labor market. In 1899 employers and workers in Denmark reached an important agreement, following months of intense industrial dispute. This compromise secured workers the right to organize, and it also established a system of collective bargaining used to this day. Similar arrangements governing the rights of employers and employees were made in other Nordic countries, resulting in what has come to be known as the Nordic model. The labor movement was also well represented politically. The Social Democrats became the largest party in the interwar period across the Nordic region. In Denmark this culminated with the party winning 46% of all votes in 1935. The first Social Democratic prime minister, Thorvald Stauning, formed a government in 1924-1926 and again in 1929-1942.[36]

As elsewhere in early twentieth-century Europe, war and crises set their mark on societal developments and on children's lives. During World War I, the Nordic countries were officially neutral and avoided direct involvement in the conflict, with the exception of Finland. Nevertheless, all three Scandinavian countries were deeply affected by the war. Many men were called up as soldiers, although most avoided combat (except men from the Danish community in Northern Schleswig, who had formally been German citizens since 1864 and were therefore forced to join the German army). The end of World War I led to the so-called re-unification of Northern Schleswig (*Sønderjylland*) with Denmark in 1920, following a referendum in the region. Re-unification greatly boosted national sentiments, which were soon manifested in art, memorial cul-

35. In Norway, women gained the right to vote in 1913; in Sweden they did so in 1921 as part of a new democratic constitution

36. In 1920, Hjalmar Branting became the first Social Democratic prime minister of Sweden; in 1928, Christopher Hornsrud from Arbeiderpartiet (the Norwegian Labour Party) became prime minister of Norway

ture, numerous songs, and revised schoolbooks. In this period, the first attempts to define children's rights were made (Lindkvist 2018).

The international economic crisis of the 1930s hit all of the Nordic countries, resulting in high unemployment rates. However, major political agreements were made in an attempt to mitigate the repercussions. In Denmark, the 1933 Kanslergade Agreement resulted in significant public investments (similar to Roosevelt's New Deal in the US) and in new social legislation based on citizens' rights to financial support from the state. This agreement is often considered a cornerstone of the Danish welfare state. Among other effects, it meant that fewer children would live in starvation and severe poverty. The cultural politics of the Social Democrats included the opening of public libraries for all citizens, including children (see below).

During the interwar period all of the Nordic countries had declared political neutrality, but World War II still affected them in different ways. Norway and Denmark were occupied by Germany in April 1940, while Sweden remained neutral.[37] In August 1943, the Danish government's collaboration with the Germans came to an end, and most of the Danish Jews managed to escape to Sweden. However, a number of Danes and Norwegians were sent to German work and concentration camps. Many children were affected because their family members were imprisoned, active in the resistance movement, or prosecuted for collaboration after Denmark's liberation on May 5, 1945. The occupation years became a major topic in the history books for generations of Danish and Norwegian children – and in books of fiction as well (Skyggebjerg 2008: 109–132).

Schools were considered important institutions in the emerging welfare states, and from 1903 the Danish school system formally ensured that all children had an opportunity to proceed to further education after the man-

37. Finland was deeply affected by World War II, with Finnish troops fighting Russian and later German troops. Many Finns lost their lives, and many fled following concessions of land to the Soviet Union in 1947 and 1948

datory seven years of elementary schooling. In practice, however, differences continued to exist between schooling in rural and urban districts, and between the opportunities available to different social classes and genders. Major school reforms were passed in 1937 and 1958, when the last remaining differences between rural and urban schools were abolished. Children's labor was increasingly regulated and prohibited – and the need for it lessened, due to the mechanization of agricultural work. This allowed more time for schooling and even gave children some spare time. The percentage of children attending school for more than seven years rose from less than 5% around 1920 to about 35% in 1950, with girls overtaking boys around the end of World War II (Appel & Coninck-Smith, vol. 4, 2013–2015: 333, 340).

Large public investments were made in school buildings and teaching materials, not least schoolbooks, and from the 1920s onwards, around 90% percent of all Danish children attended a publicly run school. Teaching was professionalized further, and in the towns female teachers outnumbered their male colleagues. New experts entered the world of schools and the lives of children: special school doctors, nurses, and dentists, school architects, and, not least, psychologists and pedagogical experts. Much inspiration came from abroad, including the US, and experimental education programs were tested to support the development of independent, creative children.

Libraries were another area of public investment and political reform. In 1905 it became possible for school libraries to apply for state funding. Even so, in 1909 it was still estimated that only 25% of Denmark's municipalities had a public collection of children's literature (Christensen 2003: 127). This changed in 1920, when an ambitious national library act was issued with the purpose of "disseminating knowledge and general enlightenment" to all citizens (*Lov om statsunderstøttede Biblioteker* 1921: 3).

The "library cause" was clearly linked to a political and democratic agenda, and the provision of books for all citizens, including children, became an official obligation in 1931. Norway specified in its Library Act of 1935 that all publicly run schools in the countryside with more than 12 pupils were to have a collection of books for children (Birkeland et al. 2005: 145). In Denmark, the first librarian who specialized in children's literature, Helga Mollerup (1900-1984), studied for a year in America at the Carnegie Library School in Pittsburgh, Pennsylvania. She explained in an interview that she had learned a lot from being among "the many nations over there" (Bertelsen 1981: 90). Upon her return to Denmark she was put in charge of the children's section at the public library visited by Tove Ditlevsen in her childhood years. The first Danish journal on children's books, *Børn og Bøger* (1948-present, "children and books"), was published by the organization of school librarians in cooperation with pioneering librarians in the field of children's literature.

Books and media in an expanding market

Min første Bog (1907, "my first book"), written by Margrethe Lønborg Jensen (1874-1944), serves as an example of a book that many Danish children would have held in their hands in the first half of the twentieth century (see p. 61). It was authorized by the school commission of Copenhagen, used in schools across the country, and published in 12 editions of 10,000 copies each between 1907 and 1955. Jens Otto Krag carried it in his school bag on his first day of school (Krag 1969: 7). The title signals that it might be the first printed book a child would own, and a feeling of ownership was encouraged on the first page, where the page layout invited children to write their own name. The text continues: "Here is a book for you! You can have it for your very own!" The cover, printed in full color in a style inspired by art nouveau, has an illustration by

Louis Moe that interweaves text and image. A solid cardboard binding with an appealing, light-green linen spine is a clear indication that the book's design had been prioritized, and that child users from all parts of society were trusted to be able to handle the valuable and beautiful object with care.

Inside the book, prose, poetry, songs with printed music, and many different kinds of illustrations reflect the author's and illustrator's interest in the interaction between image and text, thus preempting a century in which visual media would become widespread and accessible. While Jens Otto Krag was still reading the annual journal published for Christmas, *Børnenes Juleroser*, new media were gaining influence, even on printed books. Shortly after Walt Disney's *Snow White* (1937) appeared in the cinemas, a picturebook with images from the film became available, and a series of picturebooks was published with the popular child movie star Shirley Temple as the main character, including one with stills from the 1937 adaptation of the Swiss author Johanne Spyri's novel *Heidi* (1881).

Throughout the first half of the twentieth century, the Danish market for children's books continued to expand. In 1900, 21 books of prose fiction for children were published in the country, while 201 books in the same category appeared in 1945. A similar increase can be found in the number of published picturebooks, which grew from 5 titles in 1901 to 22 in 1945 (Winge 1976: 107-108). A number of surveys of Danish children's reading habits were published as well, often on the initiative of teachers or publishers. They were related to a growing interest in the quality and importance of children's reading, and perhaps also in children's opinions, as well as the potential of a growing market. Although the surveys were not conducted according to the academic research standards of later times, it is still possible to identify several trends from them. Child readers of a children's journal in the early 1900s reported

that their preferred reading was the crossover fiction from
the previous century, such as novels by Frederic Marryat,
Walter Scott, B. S. Ingemann, Harriet Beecher Stowe, and
Louisa M. Alcott. In 1919, a small survey showed a growing
interest in gendered serial novels by Danish authors, and
on one list a collection of fairytales by the Swedish author
and illustrator Elsa Beskow (1874-1953) also appeared
among the favorites (Winge 1976: 196).

Elsa Beskow's picturebooks were published across
the Nordic countries, and to some extent her illustrations
have come to represent central elements of traditional
"Nordicness". Having made her debut as an illustrator in
1897, she continued to produce an impressive number of
picturebooks that used nature and rural landscapes as the
typical setting for the narratives, with flowers and animals

as decorative elements, while still paying attention to botanical accuracy. Most of Elsa Beskow's books depict children's play and adventures in nature and combine realistic narratives with more fantastic fairytale elements, including elves and goblins. Beskow also illustrated a widely used Swedish reader, *Vil du läsa?* (1935, "do you want to read?"), authored by Herman Siegvald. Numerous copies of her books with traces of use in antiquarian bookshops, a variety of Beskow merchandise, and the fact that her books are still in print across the Nordic countries testify to the continued popularity of "the world of Beskow" in the early 2000s. In a sense, the form and content of Beskow's picturebooks represent a nostalgic approach to children, related to Romanticism and to predecessors like the British illustrator Kate Greenway, whose work was also translated and published in the Nordic countries.

Child characters and child authors

Inspiration for new trends in children's literature across the Nordic countries came from various sources. One was the American author Lucy Mitchell's *Here and Now Story Book* (1921), in which she reproduced children's own stories using their own language, inspiring similar books for young children in Sweden and Denmark (Hallberg 1996: 87). In the 1930s, Danish illustrators and authors were also inspired by exhibitions of post-revolutionary Russian avant-garde picturebooks, in which the child incarnated everything new: a new society, a new form of art, a new kind of human being uncorrupted by old ideas and structures (Weld 2014; Druker & Kümmerling-Meibauer 2015). The interaction of avant-garde circles, educators, and producers of children's literature is reflected, for instance, in the many activities of the Danish psychologist Jens Sigsgaard (1910-1991). Sigsgaard was the head of a progressive school for educators and the author of the widely translated picturebook *Palle alene i*

Verden (1942, translated as *Paul Alone in the World*). He also published articles in avant-garde art journals and promoted the works of Astrid Lindgren and other authors internationally. Sigsgaard and other public figures challenged the former hierarchy between adults and children, based on the idea that the creativity and spontaneity of children had the power to change society. Children ought to be addressed and treated as "small fellow citizens" and individuals in their own right, and questioning illegitimate authority became a key motif in books by Astrid Lindgren, among others (see below). Such progressive ideas and practices attracted much attention in contemporary debates – and in later scholarly writings – but they were neither unchallenged nor mainstream at the time.

More conservative and national values, and more traditional content and form, still characterized many publications for children, including serial novels aimed at a gender-specific market, the so-called "boys' books" and "girls' books." These series were popular across the Nordic countries. In many cases the main character in boys' books was an active, adventurous lad who either implicitly or explicitly incarnated the ideals of the scout movement. While the girls' book characters were generally linked to traditional female values, there were exceptions, such as the Bibi books by the Danish author Karin Michaëlis, in which the protagonist Bibi travels around Europe, and works by Estrid Ott, featuring lots of active, adventurous girl characters (Wegener 2021; Thrane 2015). From around 1900, historical novels for children became popular too, not least in schools, where they helped to promote the idea of Denmark as a nation with a long, coherent history (Skyggebjerg 2008).

In 1928, the major Danish newspaper *Politiken* announced that young boys could apply for a fully financed trip around the world in celebration of Jules Verne's 100th birthday. A fifteen-year-old boy named Palle Huld won the competition and embarked on a journey that took him around the world, through the UK, Canada, Japan, Russia, France, Germany, and other countries, in 44 days. In his book about his journey (Huld 1928), the young author and his probable behind-the-scenes co-authors connect the main character to his identity as a scout, and there is regular mention of his meetings with other members of the international scouting community. The idealization of the adventurous boy, who is also a trusty friend and is always in good spirits, even in the face of adversity and change, resonates with some of the qualities Campe wrote into his Robinson Crusoe character centuries earlier. Perhaps it is no coincidence that Huld's book was recommended as a suitable Christmas gift for children in 1928, alongside Defoe's novel and Beskow's picturebooks (*Social-Demokraten* 1928: 4). The international appeal of this image of boyhood is evidenced by the fact that translations of Huld's book appeared in at least 16 countries.

Creativity and imagination were qualities ascribed to the "modern child" that can be seen as a continuation of elements associated with the Romantic child (see p. 22-23). In 1944, *Politiken* announced a competition for the best picturebook produced by a child; the winner was 7-year-old Ileana Holmboe, who had written and illustrated *Urskovs-Æventyr* (1944, "jungle-adventure"), a fanciful narrative about a monkey, an elephant, and a tiger in the jungle. The illustrations were made using crayons in clear primary colors with flowers, trees, and plants playing an important role in the compositions. The book reproduced the child's handwriting, but in her preface, Ileana Holmboe also stated that her mother had helped her, so this book could be considered yet another example of co-authorship in the field of children's literature.

A final and important aspect of the modern child in children's literature from a longer-term perspective was the anti-authoritarian element in Nordic children's

books. Publishing his picturebook *Fredrik med Bilen* (1944, "Fredrik and his car") near the end of World War II, the Danish illustrator Egon Mathiesen advocated understanding across the world (and among children with different skin colors). A few years later he encouraged children to rebel against brutality and dictatorship in *Aben Osvald* (1947, translated as *Oswald the Monkey*), and gave an appraisal of tolerance in *Mis med de blå øjne* (1949, translated as *The Blue-Eyed Pussy*). The series about *Pippi Långstump* (1945–1948, translated as *Pippi Longstocking*) by Astrid Lindgren is, of course, the epitome of anti-authoritarian childhood: Pippi does very well living on her own, and chapter by chapter she questions the authority of the pillars of society, including teachers and the police. Being rich does not make her feel superior, but generous. Her physical strength does not lead her to harm anyone, but enables her to help weaker and more vulnerable members of society, including children and animals. In the first *Pippi Longstocking* and subsequent volumes, the child reader encounters language and literature as the sort of playful medium that Tove Ditlevsen enjoyed as a child. In a certain sense, Pippi also gets revenge on behalf of the young Jens Ottos of the world, when – in a humorous but also forceful manner – she ridicules the rules and regulations of traditional schooling and child-adult hierarchies, and puts adult authorities in their proper place, seen from a child character's point of view.

The growing attentiveness to the child in the first half of the twentieth century led to improved institutions for children, including schools and libraries; it also expanded and brought more variety to the market for books and other media for children. Child characters were still represented as role models, but not always by virtue of their behaving according to established norms. Sometimes their model qualities lay in their independent actions and their ability to question or even rebel against authorities. Likewise, in some cases adult mediators – remembered, real, or fictional – were authority figures in hierarchical systems, while in others they were part of more equal relationships with children. In yet other cases, like Lindgren's books about Pippi, the normal hierarchies were turned upside down. Books and other media continued to represent a variety of aesthetic and educational ideals through their form and content, whereas a medium such as film was primarily seen as providing entertainment across generations. While libraries had improved all children's access to printed media, social differences continued to play a significant role, not least in relation to the new media that were emerging.

Chapter 5.

New roles and new rights for children, 1950–2000

In the latter half of the twentieth century, children experienced the consequences of the adult debates about the access, contents, and use of media, including children's literature. Were children's literature and media to be considered art, entertainment, or a means to achieve political change, and ought children's use of them be restricted? Books and other media were made available to all children via libraries. Some voices in the debate questioned adult authority and promoted children's rights and autonomy. Towards the end of the twentieth century, cross-media phenomena became widespread, as did crossover fiction. While social realism dominated the 1970s, fantasy and mythological tales became more popular from the late 1980s onwards.

Manu, Frederik, and Rachel

The following three examples show the tremendous variety in the reading cultures of children growing up in the capital of a Nordic welfare state in the 1970s, in this case Copenhagen. The first is Manu Sareen (b. 1967), whose family immigrated to Denmark from India. He grew up in a working-class neighborhood, and later became a popular author of children's literature and a politician who served as a minister in the Danish government. Just a few kilometers away, at Amalienborg Palace, HRH Crown Prince Frederik of Denmark (b. 1968) was raised in a bilingual home, with a French father and a Danish mother, who was crowned Queen Margrethe II of Denmark in 1972. In another part of the capital, Rachel Röst (b. 1976) was brought up in a dysfunctional family in Urbanplanen, one of the city's large concrete housing estates from the late 1960s. Today, she is the founder and head of the organization *Læs for livet* ("read for your life"), which collects books and donates "libraries on demand" to children living in residential care.

According to Manu Sareen's autobiography, nobody ever read aloud to him at home (Sareen 2015: 58). In 1971, he and his mother travelled from Ludhiana in India to reunite with his father in Copenhagen, and at the local public school he attended, he was one of very few pupils with an ethnic minority background. In fifth grade, he and his classmates were told to write an essay about Hans Christian Andersen and Manu asked his father: "What do you think I should write about Hans Christian Andersen?" His father replied in Punjabi: "Who? I don't know him" (58). Manu's interest in school was limited, but after he gave a speech on the last day of school, the principal gave him a big hug and said "Manu, go out and use your life to do great things, and make us proud" (61). This left the author "with a rare feeling that someone believed I was good at something" (63). Sareen also mentions a high-school teacher and a social worker as decisive figures who provided him, as an insecure and restless young man, with support and recognition. In 2011, when he was appointed as a government minister, he had already published his first children's books, including playful adaptations of several Hans Christian Andersen tales and the first volumes of a popular, humorous series about the adventures of Iqbal Farooq, a boy with an Indian background growing up in contemporary Copenhagen (2006–2018).

At Amalienborg Palace, the young crown prince, Frederik, and his brother, Joachim, lived separately from the Queen and Prince Consort; their most regular meetings with their parents would be at the family dinners held on Sundays, or during reading sessions after dinner with their mother, Queen Margrethe. She would tell them stories from J. R. R. Tolkien's *The Lord of the Rings* (1954–1955) and read aloud from Scottish author Eric Linklater's novel *The Wind on the Moon* (1944), which she had enjoyed herself as a child. In interviews conducted for a biography about Frederik, both Joachim and Margrethe mention their shared joy in reading the Moomin novels, by the Swedish-Finnish author Tove Jansson, as their most important reading experience together. Frederik and Joachim had received the books as a present, and Joachim recalls their mother's reading aloud to them as rare "warm and happy hours" in a family life in which their parents were "not able to be parents like other parents" (Andersen 2017: 37).

In contrast, too much parental attention from her father was a problem for Rachel Röst, who grew up in the same city as Manu and Frederik. Her family belonged to the small Mormon congregation in Copenhagen, and money, food, and new clothes were scarce. Rachel's mother suffered from mental health problems, while her father tried to control all aspects of Rachel's and her sisters' lives. The Bible was not just a book; it was the set of instructions that regulated the family's life. In an interview she gave as an adult, Röst describes the local public library as "a safe haven" where she was not controlled and where she could escape her chaotic home life. Once Rachel was able to read, she read all kinds of literature, but she preferred books with strong female characters, such as Pippi Longstocking: "I was very attracted to the fact that she lived on her own without a family. She represented an open, free world, in contrast to the claustrophobic world I experienced at home" (Klog 2018). As a teenager Rachel rebelled against her parents, moved to an institution for young people, became pregnant, and gave birth to a son at the age of 19. Becoming a mother was a turning point. She resumed her education, completed an MA in comparative literature, and founded her successful, influential, and award-winning organization to support children's reading.

These brief glimpses into the childhoods of Manu, Frederik, and Rachel touch upon different kinds of engagement from teachers and parents when it comes to children's reading and education. The books read by, or to, Frederik and Rachel show that these children had access to a combination of very old texts, canonical authors, texts read generations earlier, and specific children's literature, as well as adult literature adapted for use by children.

Growing up in the welfare state

Manu's and Rachel's childhood memories give an impression of the important role played by the modern welfare state and its institutions in the lives of children growing up in the Nordic countries after World War II. Denmark and Norway had joined NATO in 1949, while Sweden and Finland remained neutral (with Finland carefully watching the politics of the USSR until the end of the Cold War). Nevertheless, the Nordic countries would often collaborate on foreign affairs, also in relation to the United Nations (UN) and international human rights issues, including the rights of children (see below). In 1973, Denmark joined the EEC (later the EU) and was followed by Sweden and Finland in 1995, while Norway remained outside the EU.

The three Scandinavian countries saw remarkable economic growth after World War II, thanks in no small part to the Marshall Plan. Their booming economies meant that more women took part-time and full-time employment outside the home. In Denmark, by 1970 the figure was around 50% of women aged 25–44, and by 1990 it was 90%.[38] This swelled the number of public kindergartens and nurseries, followed by after-school clubs (which are open both before and after school opening hours). Nine years of schooling was made mandatory in Denmark in 1972, but this had already become a reality for most children during the 1960s. Around 2000, approximately 80% of Danish children aged 0–6 attended some kind of publicly sponsored daycare (Coninck-Smith 2021: 32). The percentage of immigrant families using these institutions was not as high, but many did attend, including Manu Sareen, who writes fondly of how he soon learned to speak Danish at his kindergarten in the early 1970s. In 1980, around 3% of the Danish population had an immigrant background; in 2000 the figure was just under 10%.[39]

During the 1950s and 1960s, the social democratic parties dominated the political scene in all five Nordic countries, not least in Sweden. Even so, center-right and conservative parties would often cooperate in the development of the welfare state and its institutions, including schools, colleges, and universities. The latter are generally run without fees (for Nordic citizens), and various forms of tax-sponsored scholarships and student loans have been available from the 1970s. The so-called 1968 movement came to influence Nordic children's lives in a number of ways. This was a composite left-wing movement that emerged across Scandinavia, inspired by the American hippie movement, the students' rebellion in Paris, and later the international feminist movement. New trends in music, art, and lifestyle, including a more open attitude to sexuality and so on, had a profound impact on many

38. According to Chakravarty & Mortensen (2014: 74). On gender and the labor market across the Nordic region, see https://nordics.info/labour-markets/

39. For other Nordic countries, see https://www.nordicstatistics.org/population

educational institutions, leading to democratic initiatives such as pupils' councils in all elementary schools, and to a shift in relationships between children and adults. These were addressed in many publications for children (see below). The general political landscape was also rapidly changing, with new left-wing parties arising, but also new right-wing parties gaining influence. From the 1990s these right-wing parties were rooted in emerging criticism and hostility relating to immigration.

Not all children were equally affected by the rising standards of living or the inspiration from the 1968 movement. Nevertheless, the relatively equal distribution of wealth in the Scandinavian countries, which culminated in the 1960s and 1970s (Jensen 2021), and not least the public investments in educational and public institutions, meant that most children gained new opportunities in their access to books, media, and cultural experiences. In Denmark, new children's libraries, including library buses, were set up during the 1950s and 1960s, and the new Library Act of 1964 made it compulsory for all municipalities to provide free public libraries. This also led to the professionalization of children's literature as a field: Around 1970, children would come across professionals whose education had included instruction on children's books in daycare centers, schools, school libraries, and public libraries. The journals and newsletters of these professionals would contain reviews and debates on the subject, and during the 1970s numerous books about children's literature were published. The increase in public spending on books contributed to rising print runs at a time when the number of titles published was also growing: In 1970, around 500 children's books were published in Denmark; in 1984, that number had doubled (Weinreich 2006: 517).[40] The rising standards of living in most families was another key factor behind the expanding book market. From the 1970s, libraries were increasingly used

40. In Norway, 106 titles of children's books were registered in 1970 (fiction and textbooks, but schoolbooks not included; see Birkeland et al. 2018: 256); in Finland, 233 titles were registered in 1968 (Stockmann et al. 2000: 7); and in Sweden the much higher number of 749 titles was registered in 1970 (Tellgrenn 1982: 24). Comparisons must be made with caution, since the categories differ slightly in these sources

Children teaching each other
Children at Skolen på Islands Brygge, Copenhagen, teaching each other about the Viking Age using books and other materials. Photo from teaching experiments in the 1980s. © Stig Hasselbalch

as local "cultural centers", also allowing children to attend theater plays – often by new drama groups specializing in children's theater – and to listen to music, besides, of course, reading and borrowing books. A similar expansion and development of children's libraries occurred in all the Nordic countries.

Children's rights and influence

From the 1950s onwards, children and childhood were put on the agenda in discourses about universal rights. In 1948, the UN proclaimed the *Universal Declaration of Human Rights*, followed by the *Declaration on the Rights of the Child* in 1959, which was the predecessor of the 1989 *Convention on the Rights of the Child*. An important aspect of this convention is children's agency, including their right to be heard and have influence on their own lives. States must "assure to the child who is capable of forming his or her own views the right to express those views freely in all matters affecting the child" and the child's point of view must be "given due weight in

73

accordance with the age and maturity of the child" (Article 12). In continuation of this greater focus on children's rights, discussions have taken place in all the Nordic welfare states about the roles and responsibilities of parents and the state, respectively.

Child autonomy became a key issue in connection with the 1968 movement. For instance, the widely translated publication *Den lille røde bog for skoleelever* (1969, translated as *The Little Red Schoolbook*), by Bo Dan Andersen, Jesper Jensen, and Søren Hansen, objected to the traditional focus on duties and obedience in Danish schools and questioned the authority of teachers. The book encouraged children to ask critical questions and insist on making decisions themselves about their own education (Heywood & Strandgaard Jensen 2018). In the course of the late 1960s and 1970s, most teachers went from being addressed as, say, "Miss Jensen", "Mrs. Hansen" or "Mr. Andersen" to being called by their first names. Corporal punishment by teachers in Denmark was forbidden in 1967 – although that did not stop Manu Sareen from receiving disciplinary slaps on the head in the 1970s (Sareen 2015: 58). Not until 1997 did it become entirely illegal for Danish parents to physically discipline their children – much later than in Sweden (1979), and Norway (1987). During the latter half of the 1900s, there was also more focus on children's mental well-being. A certification program for school psychologists was established in Denmark in 1965, reflecting the new attention being paid to children with special needs. Near the end of the century, an awareness of children as individuals and theories about multiple intelligences and learning styles increased the interest that adults and professionals were taking in child psychology, including newly defined diagnoses such as Attention Deficit Hyperactivity Disorder (ADHD) and Asperger's Syndrome.

Increased access to books and media

The *Convention on the Rights of the Child* points explicitly to children's right to access information, media, books, and cultural experiences. In the 1970s, children could listen to music and borrow LP records at libraries, and later they could borrow CDs and VHS video tapes. The Norwegian author Thorbjørn Egner (1912-1990) had begun his career in the 1940s by telling and singing his own stories and songs to children on NRK, Norway's national broadcasting corporation. These stories were later *remediated* – transferred to another medium – as books, theater plays, and LPs, and translated into all Nordic languages. In 1948, Astrid Lindgren adapted her *Pippi Longstocking* (1945) into a stage version, and later into a popular television series that was broadcast across the Nordic countries from 1969. The national Nordic broadcasting corporations had all set up children's departments around 1950. In the early history of Danish children's television, acclaimed illustrators such as Egon Mathiesen, Jørgen Clevin, and Ib Spang Olsen were engaged in a combined effort to entertain, educate, and introduce children to the art of drawing. The anti-authoritarian, experimental tendencies of the 1968 movement arrived at DR, the Danish broadcasting corporation, with the appointment in 1968 of a new director in charge of the child and youth department, Mogens Vemmer, who was keen on engaging children directly in the content-production process.

Around 1970, several well-established Danish publishing houses developed separate and thriving departments for children's books. Gyldendal published prominent Nordic authors, while Høst & Søn became one of the front-runners in the publication of progressive and more politically motivated children's literature, such as books written by Swedish author Sven Werntröm (1925-2018). Across the Nordic countries, he was popular among the

"1968 generation" teachers, librarians, and parents with titles such as *Kamrat Jesus* (1971, "comrade Jesus") and the historical series *Trälarne* (1973, "the serfs").

The efforts to increase children's access to books and media brought discussions about quality and content in their wake. All Nordic countries witnessed debates about the need to protect children from harmful content, weighed against their right to choose and decide for themselves. During the 1950s, intense debates revolved around the fear that depictions of violence and sex in comic books would lead to copy-cat behavior (Strandgaard Jensen 2017). In the 1980s, with the arrival of the "home video", similar discussions arose about films. The closest Denmark has ever come to a book ban on children's literature was in 1976, when a public library refused to purchase the prize-winning young adult novel *Katamaranen* (1976, "the catamaran") by Bent Haller, which included swearing, an episode depicting sexual harassment among children, and a young man committing suicide (Weinreich 2015: 63). In Denmark, films were (and are) the most strictly regulated medium, and the national film council set the age limit at 12 when Olle Hedman's film adaptation of Astrid Lindgren's *Bröderna Lejonhjärta* (1977, translated as *The Brothers Lionheart*) was first shown in movie theaters.

The broad public interest in the quality of children's literature and the attention paid to children's literature published in the Nordic languages were reflected in the announcement of national children's books awards in Norway in 1948, Sweden in 1950, and Denmark in 1954. Academic research into children's literature and media was also gradually developing, first in Sweden, where Svenska Barnboksinstitutet – a center for the study and dissemination of knowledge about children's books – was founded in 1965,[41] and the first professorial chair for children's literature was announced in 1982 at Stockholm University.

41. The Finnish Institute for Children's Literature was founded in 1978, the Norwegian Institute for Children's Literature in 1979, and the Danish Centre for Children's Literature (today the Centre for Children's Literature and Media) in 1998

From social realism to fantasy

Various aspects of children's literature in this period point to growing respect for the child – as a producer and intended audience. Walking the main street in Copenhagen in the 1970s, one might have come across a man in a remarkable, colorful outfit selling a small pamphlet entitled *Hindbærbrus og Kragetæer* (1968–1971, "raspberry fizz and chicken scratches") from a cheerfully decorated baby buggy. The street vendor Otto Sigvaldi (1943–2015) was also the editor and publisher of this pamphlet-style journal, and in the introduction to the first issue he promoted children's own writing in their own words. The preface also stated that the stories were written and illustrated by children aged 7–13, and it encouraged children to submit texts for future issues. Like the inclusion of children in television production processes, Sigvaldi's publication was one of several initiatives in which children were engaged as co-producers of texts and media for children in the 1970s. Sigvaldi's small journal consisted of 16 pages stapled together in a cardboard binding, so the publication shares elements with the cheap and simple chapbooks sold by peddlers and read by children in earlier centuries. In Sigvaldi's case, the illustrations of the narratives were humorous drawings made by himself or by child contributors, and most of the stories were characterized by inventiveness, relatively free association, and a lack of concern about unity of time, place, and action.

The debate about comic books had died out by the 1970s, and translations of especially French-language series such as *Asterix*, *Tintin*, and *Lucky Luke* were available in libraries. Meanwhile, the book in the form of a classical codex (see p. 9) was still a popular medium and, at the same time, sometimes an exclusive one. When Astrid Lindgren published *Ronja rövardotter* (1981, translated as *Ronja the Robber's Daughter*), the book was equipped with a dust jacket and hardcover binding, printed on high-quality paper, and richly illustrated, including a full-color cover illustration and decorated endpapers, all signaling that children deserve well-designed, well-crafted books made with high aesthetic ambitions. The black-and-white drawings by Ilon Wikland were an integral part of the book. On the cover, Wikland portrayed the main character, the child Ronja, as a barefooted hunter at home in nature, gazing at the birds around her and set against a fairytale castle in the background.

The character Ronja combines elements of a modern, agentive, independent, anti-authoritarian girl with elements of the sensitive and sometimes lonely child well known from Lindgren's other narratives. The story tells how Ronja and a boy named Birk are born into rival robbers' gangs, and how they manage not only to become close companions, but also to unite their two families. Much of the narrative takes place in the forest, where Ronja and Birk go to escape the conflicts of their families, and it combines fairytale elements and a Romeo

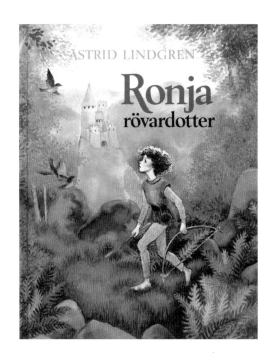

and Juliet-style story line with fantastical elements. The content reflects Lindgren's continuous interest in showing that children should be respected in their own right, especially since they are more sensible in their actions and thoughts than adults. Four decades later, this book is still being published in a very similar design, although a version with illustrations based on the Japanese animated version by Katsuya Kondo is also available. Moreover, the book has been adapted into a movie and a musical, and while Ronja was an unusual name in the 1980s, by 2020 it had become quite common in the Nordic region.[42]

From the 1950s onwards, across the Nordic countries attention was drawn to playful and formal aspects of children's texts in the nonsensical poetry of Inger Hagerup (Norway), Lennart Hellsing (Sweden), and Halfdan Rasmussen (Denmark). In prose, an increased appreciation of the literary qualities of children's texts was reflected in

42. In 2020, according to the national statistics agencies, 6,908 girls and women in Sweden bear the name Ronja, along with 2,389 in Norway and 1,608 in Denmark; cf. scb.se, ssb.no, and dst.dk

children's books by the Danish author Cecil Bødker, whose series about the adventures of an independent boy in *Silas og den sorte hoppe* (1967, translated as *Silas and the Black Mare*), set in a non-specific, archaic setting, was republished in 2017. Swedish authors Gunnel Linde, famous for *Den vita stenen* (1964, "the white stone"), and Marie Gripe share with Bødker the aim and the ability to depict children's feelings and experiences in precise and carefully elaborate language. These characteristics are pivotal in the works of the Swedish-Finnish author and illustrator Tove Jansson (1914–2001), whose Moomin books, set in a mythical valley landscape filled with a community of extraordinary characters, continue to be published, translated, and remediated (Westin 2014).

From the 1970s onwards, picturebooks began to reflect changing family structures. In the Swedish author and illustrator Gunilla Bergström's picturebook series about *Alfons Åberg* (1972–2012, translated as *Alfie Atkins*, with 24 different titles), the main character lives with his father, and the series takes the daily concerns of young children quite seriously – but with a humorous twinkle in the author's eye. The series is one of relatively few picturebooks from the 1970s that is still in print and has been widely translated. Other picturebooks published across Nordic countries showed child characters experiencing their parents divorcing, and in 1981 Susanne Bösche published the first Danish picturebook featuring a girl who lives with two male parents, *Mette bor hos Morten og Erik* (1981, translated as *Jenny lives with Eric and Martin*).[43] Being open and outspoken about contested aspects of life or society and "weighty" topics such as death, unemployment, or environmental problems was considered a part of treating children with respect in Nordic children's literature from the 1970s onwards. During the same period, a tendency to write directly and explicitly about young people addressing issues of love, sex, pregnancy, and abortion

43. The English translation became the center of a highly politicized discussion in the UK in 1988 about books as an endorsement of homosexuality

was strongly manifested in fiction for young adults. Such realistic young adult fiction became a supplement to the traditional and popular "girls' books" and "boys' books" series published in previous decades.

Reading aloud continued to be part of the reading culture in many homes, and during the 1970s and 1980s one of the most widely read Danish authors was the teacher and author Ole Lund Kirkegaard, who subscribed to the same anti-authoritarian ideals as many contemporary authors, and who shared his humorous and ironic inversion of power relations between children and adults with Astrid Lindgren. A renewed interest in Nordic mythology, across the Nordic countries and internationally, was reflected in the numerous translations of Lars-Henrik Olsen's series about *Erik Menneskesøn* (1986–2006, translated as *Erik, Son of Man*), which combined an introduction to Nordic mythology with a fictional narrative framework. Olsen did this without the underlying patriotism and nationalism of historical fiction seen in earlier decades. From the late 1980s, a modern sort of fairytale novel that included mythical and fantastical elements was developed, among many others by the Danish authors Josefine Ottesen, Lene Kaaberbøl, and Cecilie Eken, who preceded the flood of fantasy novels that followed the publication of J. K. Rowling's first book about Harry Potter in 1997.[44]

Translated books were also an important part of children's reading in this period. The international canon of children's literature included books from the English Golden Age, with several illustrated editions of works like Lewis Carroll's *Alice in Wonderland* (1865) and A. A. Milne's *Winnie-the-Pooh* (1926) on the market. Detective stories by Enid Blyton were also read by Nordic children for decades, and were relaunched in Denmark around 2020 in slightly adapted versions with new covers. Lisa Tetzner's books about a group of children in Berlin before, during, and after WW II, *Die Kinder aus Nr. 67* ("the children of no.

44. *Harry Potter and the Philosopher's Stone* (1997) was published in Danish on January 1, 1998 (as *Harry Potter og De Vises Sten*), six months after the English original. The first version in Swedish was published in 1999

67"), originally published in German in 1933-1949, were republished in Denmark as late as 1984, and ever since its first publication, German author Michael Ende's *Momo* (1981) has continuously been on the market. Another international bestseller, and steady seller, was the Norwegian author Jostein Gaarder's book *Sofies verden* (1991, translated as *Sophie's World*), an introduction for young readers to the history of philosophy. Although there was a certain focus on the importance of broadening children's horizons geographically, and although many fact-oriented and often photo-illustrated books for children would tell about the lives of children in Africa and Asia, very few fictional books for children coming from outside a Western context were translated into Nordic languages. A rare example of a successful book series with a main character from a minority background was the Swedish author Katarina Taikon's autobiographical series about the Roma girl Katitzi, originally published in 1969-1980, which was widely translated and is still in print in many countries (Widhe 2021).

Towards the end of the twentieth century, digital technologies made children's book production much cheaper. Especially the production of picturebooks benefited from this development, with full-color books becoming the norm during the 1990s. While children's access to books through public institutions had improved, the variety of genres and media had also increased, leading to discussions around the turn of the millennium about Danish children lacking the time and the motivation to read books (Steffensen & Weinreich 2001). At the same time, children benefited – and perhaps in some cases also suffered – from the intensified attention on all aspects of their lives, including their reading habits and media consumption.

Chapter 6.

Autonomous children in a global world after 2000

Globalization and digitization, often combined, are deeply impacting children's literature and children's media use in a wide variety of ways. Children access and produce content on digital platforms, but at the same time the materiality of the book is being explored. Global changes, as evident, for instance, in climate change and migration, are reflected in narratives for children. Books and other media interact in numerous ways, often with children as co-creators. Nordic children today are growing up in more diverse welfare states, where more institutionalization has led to some homogenization of childhoods, but where signs of a widening divide between privileged and less privileged children are also apparent. Children's use of books and other media is still occurring through different child-adult interactions, and also in various types of national and international productions.

Nordic children in a globalized world

The societies in which Nordic children are growing up in the early twenty-first century are shaped by strong continuities that are linked to the history presented on the preceding pages.[45] All five Nordic countries are liberal democracies, and Denmark, Sweden, and Norway are still constitutional monarchies, while Iceland and Finland are republics. Lutheran Protestantism has remained the dominating religion across the region, but while Sweden, Norway, and Finland no longer have a state church, the evangelical Lutheran church holds a privileged position as a de facto state church in Denmark and Iceland. Despite differences in their affiliation with international institutions such as NATO and the EU (see p. 70), the Nordic countries share a number of communal platforms and organizations, including the Nordic Council, established in 1952 as an interparliamentary body for political and cultural cooperation. In 2013 this council established a Nordic prize for children's literature to strengthen the focus on common elements in the region's books for children. This decision was clearly influenced by an awareness of increasingly strong international and transnational influences on children's lives and media in a globalized world.

In 2015, the Danish news media were full of press photos of Syrian refugees walking along Danish highways in their attempt to flee the war in their native country. Danish soldiers have been, and still are, taking part in international operations, such as the recently retracted US-led force that entered Afghanistan after 9/11 – the terrorist attack on the Twin Towers in New York City in 2001. Various media designed for children try to explain the impact of such global conflicts to Danish children. On the cover of *Børneavisen* (2018–present, "the children's newspaper"), a weekly print newspaper published by the media house JP/Politiken, the following headlines could be seen in the

45. Population figures in 2020 are approximately four to five times larger than in 1820 (see p. 37): in Denmark, 5.8 million; Norway, 5.4 million; Sweden, 10.3 million; Finland, 5.4 million; and Iceland, 357,000. Cf. https://www.norden.org/en/information/facts-about-nordic-countries

autumn of 2020: "Read why wearing a mask can be a good idea" (August 11, 2020), and "Conrad collects trash for world clean-up day" (September 29, 2020), highlighting the global challenges of climate change, and the COVID-19 pandemic that changed the everyday lives of children around the world from January 2020.

The media house behind *Børneavisen* is also the publisher of the national newspaper *Jyllands-Posten*, which in 2005 published an article that included caricatures of the Prophet Muhammad. The article was linked to an interview with the Danish children's book author Kåre Bluitgen, who stated that he had had difficulty finding an illustrator for a children's book about the Prophet Muhammad for children, since within Islam there is no tradition of depicting the face of the Prophet. Subsequently, *Jyllands-Posten* asked illustrators to draw the Prophet as a statement, allegedly to promote the right to free speech. The publication of the resulting drawings ignited a global conflict that included flag-burnings and attacks on Danish embassies, but which also led to ongoing discussions in Denmark about the need to respect sensitive issues among religious minorities. Bluitgen's children's book about the Prophet Muhammad was published in 2006 with illustrations by an anonymous illustrator (Bluitgen 2006).

The tensions concerning these drawings – a situation often referred to as "the cartoon controversy" – are related to the fact that Nordic children today are growing up in much more diverse societies than their parents and grandparents did. Around 2020, the Nordic populations include descendants of the "guest workers" from the 1960s, refugees and asylum seekers from global conflicts, and children of migrant workers, especially from other Nordic countries and Europe. In all the Nordic countries, immigration policies have become a topic of heated debate. This is a more recent development in Sweden, where ideas of a more multicultural society have generally been more widely embraced. In Denmark, on the other hand, a discourse about foreigners' insufficient integration into a monocultural norm of *danskhed* (Danishness) was launched by a right-wing party in the 1990s and became increasingly mainstream during the 2000s and 2010s. A political preoccupation with Danish national identity was reflected in the launching of a "national canon" for school curriculums in 2004, including a list of must-read Danish authors for publicly run schools. Currently, Tove Ditlevsen, one of our childhood reader examples, is one of only two women on the list (*Dansk - Fælles Mål* 2019: 14).

While children in the welfare states of the Nordic region rarely risk lacking food, housing, clothing, or medical care, or have to take employment to co-support their own families, many of them face a variety of social and psychological challenges. Increasing economic inequality, especially but not exclusively experienced by children who have what is sometimes politically termed "another ethnic origin than Danish," means that a growing number of children live in relative poverty (Coninck-Smith 2021: 30). Across all social groups, more children are now being given psychiatric diagnoses – with some uncertainty as to whether this has to do with an actual increase in cases, or can be attributed to growing awareness in this field. Children's welfare is still a concern in the Nordic welfare states, and it is often high on the political agenda, including funding for specific interventions to support vulnerable children growing up in families suffering abuse, violence, or neglect. Children's rights are frequently debated in discussions about regulations of new reproductive technologies and sexuality: Do children have a right to know who their biological parents are, which might make in vitro reproduction via donors more difficult? Does a young child have the right to choose his or her own gender identity, including making decisions to begin hormone treatment at a young age? These and similar questions reflect the continuous debates on children's agency.

Books, media, and changing institutions

Computers became widespread in Nordic households in the years around 2000, followed by smartphones and tablets around 2010; children have thus experienced a remarkable increase in their access to entertainment, information, and aesthetic experiences, and also to means of producing content themselves via digital media and platforms. In 2020, YouTube was the platform used by the largest number of Danish children (Hansen 2021). The vast majority have access to computers, smartphones, and tablets, often owning their own personal devices – which made it possible, during the COVID-19 pandemic of 2020–2021, to replace in-school teaching for all age groups with online teaching. Since the breakthrough of tablets and smartphones, many publishers of children's books have feared this would mean the end of the book in the form of the traditional codex, but that has not been the case. In Denmark, the annual number of novels and short stories published for children in Danish has increased from 1,126 in 2010 to 1,675 in 2019 (Starup & Jensen 2020: 10).[46] Schools and public libraries are still important purchasers of books and digital content for children, and during the 2010s, digital portals became widely used in schools. The education departments of major publishing houses such as Gyldendal and Egmont produce and sell digital access to educational material, both to literature previously published in the codex format and to texts that were "born digitally".

A general tendency in the publishing industry to centralize has also affected the production of children's books. For instance, Høst & Søn (see p. 75) became part of Gyldendal in 2019. However, new Nordic publishers continue to emerge, and several new, small publishers

46. Information about similar figures in Norway and Sweden can be found on the websites of the Norwegian and the Swedish institutes for children's books (www.barnbokinstituttet.no and www.barnboksinstitutet.se)

are focusing on experimental, high-quality children's literature that also finds its way into schools. In recent decades, picturebooks and graphic novels have become an integrated part of the curriculum in Danish schools, which may have to do with greater focus in the official guidelines on visual literacy and multimodal texts. Some small presses specialize in books that focus on diversity, such as the Swedish publisher Olika (meaning "different").

Digitization has increased children's options for accessing narratives and information through a variety of media and modes of expression. The Danish author Camilla Hübbe and the illustrator Ramus Meisler have published two narratives that each bear the name of their main character – *Tavs* (2012, "silent") and *Nord* (2017, "north"). Although designed in digital, animated versions meant to be read on a tablet or computer, *Tavs* and *Nord* also appeared as graphic novels in the codex format. *Nord* was set in Iceland, revolved around Nordic identity in a global world, was supported by the Nordic Council, and was also translated into Icelandic (Henkel 2021). The digital version of *Tavs* bears some resemblance to computer games, which have become a very important part of children's lives since the late 1990s. The borders between literature and computer games are being explored in new, digitally born narratives that challenge traditional definitions of literature as written and printed text (Mygind & Poulsen 2018). Through public libraries, children also have access to digital books and audiobooks, a service which was used even more than usual by both children and adults during the COVID-19 pandemic. Recent research into children's reading culture across media shows that children's interest in specific narratives transcends media: When asked which narratives they have found most interesting, children refer to books as well as movies (Henkel et al. forthcoming). Digital platforms have increased children's opportunities to produce and share fiction and fan-fiction. One of the most popular sites is the transnational platform Movellas, launched in Denmark, where narratives by young authors are published, sometimes widely read, and commented on by children and young people themselves.

Owned by international companies across the world, media and platforms such as YouTube, Facebook, Instagram, and TikTok allow children to become (co)producers of content in dialogue with existing media. Since early childhood, a young Danish YouTuber named Naja Münster has been co-producing content for children on YouTube, and later on Instagram and TikTok as well, based at her home in a small provincial town (Johansen 2021). Beginning in 2019, Naja Münster became the main character in a series of Danish children's books for tween girls written by the children's book author Line Kyed (2019), and Naja's followers on YouTube could share her delight at "unboxing" her copies of the first volumes.

Many children use international video streaming services, but the majority of Danish children and parents also use the platforms provided by the national public-service broadcaster DR (Hansen & Scheutz 2021). This is regarded as an important means of promoting – and conserving – Nordic ideas of childhood, and stimulating children's language acquisition of their mother tongue. International debates on Danish-produced content for children regularly arise, as was the case in 2020, when YouTube banned content from DR that was considered offensive from an American point of view. In such debates, Nordic media scholars often stress that Nordic texts and media for children are based on ideas of a competent, anti-authoritarian child with a carnivalesque sense of humor that is related to their play culture (Lundtofte 2021). One way children and adults continue to share narratives is through the popular Christmas tradition of special "advent calendars" (*julekalendere*): Nordic national and commercial television stations produce 24 episodes, with one aired daily throughout December, leading up to Christmas Eve, and often they contain intertextual and intermedial references that reach out to viewers across generations.

The role of public libraries and school libraries is central to recurring debates about children's interest in reading. Surveys show that Nordic children, especially boys, have a relatively low motivation for or engagement in reading as such, and concerns about children's reading abilities seem to be constant, especially in relation to the biannual international PISA surveys conducted in the schools. The PISA survey in 2018 indicated that 16% of 15-16-year-old Danish pupils had very poor reading skills (Christensen 2019: 9). Huge differences in young people's readings habits are reflected in a recent survey showing that while around 15% of 12-19-year-olds never read fiction, 40% of their age group read fiction weekly or even more often (Starup & Jensen 2020: 45–46).

In Denmark, public libraries are challenged by the fact that children's school days have become longer – and by children's ability to access information, entertainment, and aesthetic experiences in many other ways. Additional concern among professionals with an interest in literature was caused by the official renaming of the "school library" (*skolebibliotek*) to the "center for learning" (*læringscenter*), reflecting the increased focus on cross-media education and potentially decreasing the attention paid to books and literature. However, the most recent survey of children's reading habits in Denmark shows that many turn to school librarians when they need information about what to read – and also to their peers and their mothers (Reinholdt Hansen 2018). On platforms such as bookeaters.dk, hosted by the Danish public libraries, children are encouraged to recommend books to each other.

As for the use of children's books in kindergartens, a recent research article examines policy documents and guidelines across the Nordic countries and discusses these in relation to the Nordic preschool tradition. The authors conclude that the training of kindergarten teachers could be improved in order to "enable children to become active participants in their reading communities" based on their own interests (Hogsnes et al. 2020: 15-16).

Trends in current children's literature

As of 2020, most Nordic children have access to narratives in digital and analogue media from a very young age. The standard format of a book for infants (1–2 years old) has been a hardcover book measuring around 14 x 14 cm, consisting of 12 double spreads, as it has been ever since such books began to appear on the Scandinavian market in the 1940s in a design specially developed for the youngest book users. When reading such books with their parents, small children acquire media literacy and proficiency in using the codex format, as well as confronting fiction in the most basic Aristotelian sense: A character progresses through an invented plot consisting of a beginning, a middle, and an end. Today's children can experience the exact same narrative on their tablet, for instance in the author Peter Nordahl and the illustrator Rasmus Bregnhøi's series starring a dog named Ib, which is available as a codex version and an e-book via iTunes. The e-book version also contains a simple Ib computer game. The e-book enables children to listen to the author reading aloud in a deep, melodic voice; they can thereby learn to access and "read" the narrative without direct adult intervention. Parents may also buy a small bag containing a number of (analogue) Ib books, thereby gaining portable access to a number of Ib-themed stories. When choosing this version, they do not have to charge the battery of their tablets, whereas the tablet and smartphone versions give access to an almost infinite number of narratives. Children can also see and hear the author and illustrator sing the Ib song, or watch the author perform Ib narratives in

Reading aloud – on social media
A photo of a mother reading aloud to her son from one of Rasmus Bregnhøi and Peter Nordahl's books about "Ib the dog". Posted on Instagram in 2020. © Lene Huldgaard Boe

daycare centers as a puppet theater show. In 2021, Ib movies also became accessible through Paramount's streaming service.

Interestingly, the digital turn has also led to a renewed interest in the book as a medium. Illustrators, authors, publishers, and graphic designers seem to share an interest in presenting and drawing attention to the specific qualities of the codex, especially in relation to tactile and visual elements. Covers are decorated and shaped in remarkable ways, reflecting the content and genres of the narratives, and fully illustrated books printed on high-quality paper are equipped with details such as colored ribbons as bookmarks. Inside the books, the graphic design often encourages the reader to interact with the book, turn it around in order to follow twists in text and illustration, or open fold-out elements in new variations of what is known as "the drama of the turning of the page"

(Nikolajeva & Scott 2001). Playful experiments include book objects such as Mette Hegnhøj's *Emma er mit navn vil du købe det* (2014, "Emma is my name would you like to buy it"), which was published as a handmade "type-written" manuscript in a box with a number of significant tactile elements related to the narrative, set in an antiquarian bookshop. Subsequently, the book object was re-mediated and adapted into a codex, for use in schools and for dissemination through libraries (Linkis 2019).

Another significant change in the physical appearance of children's books is the growing number of fully illustrated publications. Previously, illustrated books were considered a medium for smaller children who were not yet able to read, but today illustrations seem to be an asset for any publication, and new digital technologies have generally made book production cheaper and the printing of full-color illustrations profitable for publishers. The boundaries between comic books and picturebooks are becoming blurred, and around 2020 a number of publications challenge established genre categories. Many books are promoted as graphic novels, a denominator which currently seems to cover fully illustrated, bound books that combine elements of comics and picturebooks while telling a fictional, visual-verbal narrative of significant length. The contents of these narratives often revolve around emotional difficulties among friends and families, but they also deal with a number of complex global topics such as climate change, migration, and refugees, or even sexual abuse. One reason for this could be that the image-text interaction creates a more open space for thought and interpretation on the part of the reader.

One example of how the attentiveness to image-text interaction leaves room for reader reflection is the graphic novel *Zenobia* (2016), by the Danish author Morten Dürr and the illustrator Lars Hornemann. This was one of several Nordic books published in connection with the focus on Syrian refugees. On the initial pages of the book, the reader meets Amina, a young Syrian girl who is alone in a crowded boat on the Mediterranean. The book then cross-cuts between the situation at sea and the girl's former quiet family life, her fleeing her home, and narratives told by her mother about the ancient female warrior queen Zenobia. On the last pages, the reader watches Amina drown. So far, the book has been translated into more than 16 languages. Furthermore, it has been remediated into a theater play.

Zenobia reflects a growing desire to represent a more diverse society in children's books. Similarly influenced by international discussions about diversity in the media and cultural products, especially in the United States, young Nordic citizens are paying more attention than their parents and grandparents to issues of ethnicity,[47] gender, and sexuality. This is reflected in books by young authors, but also in debates about aspects of the canonical Nordic literature that can be considered offensive from a modern point of view. The call for tolerance and universalism in the works of canonical authors such as Thorbjørn Egner, Egon Mathiesen, and Astrid Lindgren was explicit when their books were published, but today adjustments of specific expressions are being made – or at least discussed. For instance, the use of the Swedish word "negerkung" ("negro-king") in Lindgren's Pippi books has been changed in recent editions in Sweden, Norway, and Denmark (Ommundsen 2021). The depiction of a certain female character in Thorbjørn Egner's work and his song about "Hottentots" have sparked debates across the Nordic region. Likewise, when a number of poems with stereotypical depictions of Black and Chinese children were not reprinted in a new edition of the canonical nonsense poet Halfdan Rasmussen's work, generational differences became obvious. Older readers tended to point to Rasmussen's aim of fostering tolerance and international under-

47. One of the main differences here between the Nordic countries, some European countries, and the US is the attitude towards "race", which in a European context is problematic due to the use of the term during the Nazi regime; see Capshaw (2021)

48. For a discussion
of such cases in a
US context, see Nel
(2017)

standing, while younger generations pointed to the fact
that the stereotypes were nevertheless offensive.[48]

In Sweden and Norway, scholarly attention has
been drawn in recent years to children's texts by minority authors and to books about a more ethnically diverse
society. The Swedish anthology *Mångkulturell barn- och
ungdomslitteratur* (2017, "multicultural children's and
young adult literature"), by Andersson & Druker, is one
example, and a Norwegian survey has since examined a
wide range of aspects of multicultural children's literature
in Norway (Ørjasæter & Johnsen 2021). In Denmark, new
research discusses the use of multicultural literature in
Danish schools and compares US and Danish approaches
to multicultural children's literature (Mansour & Martin
2020).

The need for a new generation to address questions concerning Denmark's colonial past and postcolonial
challenges is reflected in the Danish-Greenlandic author
Niviaq Korneliussen's novel *Homo Sapienne* (2014), which
follows a group of urban youth in the Greenlandic capital of Nuuk. The interaction between Inuit tradition and
global culture manifests itself in the way the young characters relate to their local cultural heritage and to the global
English-language music culture, even while touching on
the challenges that contemporary Greenlandic society
faces in dealing with alcohol, abuse, and a high suicide rate.
Homo Sapienne was received as a literary work for adults
and as young adult fiction, and the tendency to address
a less specific audience across generations is widespread
in Nordic children's literature (Westin 2004). In Norway
and Sweden, the term *all-alder litteratur* ("literature for all
ages") was used before the English term "crossover literature" became widespread (Ommundsen 2015). The fact
that identity, including age, is understood in terms of a
continuum rather than as a series of binary contradictions

might be one reason why publishers and authors often address less specific age groups and readerships.

A return to descriptions of exemplary characters in fiction and non-fiction is evident, not only in the Nordic countries, but also internationally. Two young women have become icons and role models in twenty-first-century global debates: the Pakistani promoter of girls' rights Malala Yousafzai (b. 1997) and the Swedish climate activist Greta Thunberg (b. 2003). After speaking publicly about girls' rights to education, Malala was shot by the Taliban, hospitalized in the UK, and, upon her recovery, awarded the Nobel Peace Prize in 2014. Subsequently, her life story was told in an autobiography for adults, an adapted book for children, a movie, and even a number of widely translated picturebooks and illustrated textbooks for children. In Sweden, another millennial started her career as a climate activist at the age of 15 with "school strikes" every Friday in front of the Swedish parliament. Greta Thunberg has since become an international icon and an advocate for a fundamental change in climate policies, who was invited to speak at the UN assembly in 2018. Today, portrayals of Thunberg and Yousafzai are included in numerous collections of biographies of children who have "changed the world." While there is a long tradition of narratives of exemplary lives in children's literature, today the agentic, courageous child who raises her voice and uses her body to fight injustice seems to incarnate and be (re)presented as a dominant educational ideal and a role model worth following. On the cover of a recent Danish example of such a collection, the American "March for our lives" activist Emma Gonzales is depicted in front of Nice Nailantei Leng'ete, the young Kenyan activist for girls' rights not to be circumcised, and Greta Thunberg.

Climate change as a global challenge and also as a concern of children growing up in the Nordic countries is evidenced by the large number of children's books ad-

dressing this theme. The scholarly anthology *Ecocritical Perspectives on Children's Texts and Cultures: Nordic Dialogues* (Goga et al. 2018) discusses whether there is a special Nordic approach to questions about the relationship between human beings and nature, a special type of Nordic nature, and specific ideas concerning the education of eco-critical citizens in the Nordic region. By wearing a yellow raincoat, the main character in Søren Jessen's graphic novel *Fiskepigen* (2020, "the fishgirl") makes a bow to Greta Thunberg, and the narrative develops around her fight against the flooding of her house. Similar interests across the Nordic borders are reflected in the picture-book *Om du möter en björn* (2021, "if you meet a bear"), by Kivela, Serup, & Bondestam, which is based on cross-Nordic collaboration addressing the power relationship between nature and human beings in a humorous way.

Slimfjorden (2021, "the slimefiord"), by the Danish author Sarah Lang Andersen and the Danish-Faroese illustrator Kathrina Skarðsá, highlights a child's concern with local environmental problems in a combination of gravity and humor, as an old wolf, a moose arriving from Sweden, and a fluorescent jellyfish from the United States point to local, regional, and international aspects of climate change.

As relatively small countries with national languages spoken by small populations, Sweden, Norway, and Denmark all have national funding programs to support and publish translations, including of children's literature, and many translations are still produced across the Nordic countries. The Norwegian illustrator and author Stian Hole has become very popular in Denmark, and his innovative use of digital collages, his compassionate texts that focus on children's feelings, and his selectiveness when choosing authors to illustrate have brought him world renown. Recently, he chose to illustrate texts by the Danish author Kim Fupz Aakeson, who shares his subtle humor and gentle irony. Aakeson's own stories, for instance his series about the boy Vitello (2008–present), also seem to travel well, with titles such as *Vitello går med kniv* (2008, translated as *Vitello carries a knife*). While the title might seem surprising – and perhaps inappropriate – in a US context, the thick irony would be obvious in a Danish context, as carrying a knife in public spaces is forbidden for everyone, regardless of age, unless you happen to be a scout in uniform, for instance, or an angler on a fishing trip (*Knivloven* 2016, "the Danish knife act"). Recently, Asian countries, including China, have become a new market for the publishing of Nordic children's literature, especially picturebooks. At the same time, Nordic children continue to appreciate the increasing number of transmedia products designed for children, which release books, computer games, films, and merchandise simultaneously for an international market (Mygind 2019).

Chapter 7.
Conclusions

In this book, brief outlines of the reading cultures of Friederike, Hans Christian, Anton, Ida, Tove, Jens Otto, Manu, Frederik, and Rachel have pointed to continuities and also to changes and composite chronologies in the history of children's access to literature and media in the Nordic world – with Denmark as our key example. Their reading and media practices show that some elements are relatively constant and appear to be "themes with variations," while others are related to momentous changes in society, in media technologies, in the perceptions of childhood, and in the forms and contents of children's literature in the broadest sense of the word.

For over 250 years, the book as a medium, the codex, has been a constant source of education, entertainment, and aesthetic experience, for children as well as adults. The overall design of this medium has been remarkably stable: It has consisted of inscribed pages, sewn or glued together, and surrounded by a binding, from the printed ABCs held in the hands of most eighteenth-century Nordic children to the digitally designed and industrially produced books read by children today. The most obvious change in the codex is that illustrations have become an integrated part of most books published. However, while the codex itself has been relatively stable, its surroundings have not.

By following these child figures, we have been able to show how books have interacted with other media and modes of expression across centuries. Children do not only read books specifically written for them, and they combine the reading of books with experiencing fiction and information through tales told orally, illustrated broadsheets, drama, puppet theater, wall charts, journals and magazines, radio, comic books, film, television, video, computers, tablets, or smartphones. While some of these media are no longer used or produced, new media continue to be introduced into children's lives. Composite and changing media usage is, to some extent, an old phenomenon, but evidently, dramatic changes have taken place: For centuries, books were the dominating medium for literature that targeted children, whereas today they are just one of many media specifically produced *for* children.

Children's engagement in the media they use can also be traced down through the centuries. Our miniature portraits show that not only privileged children like Friederike and Ida, but also some children from less privileged backgrounds, such as Hans Christian and Anton, would actively seek to influence their own access to literature and media. Whereas most children in the late eighteenth and early nineteenth centuries had limited access to texts and media produced explicitly for them, Hans Christian and Anton managed to compose a diverse literary diet that represented different genres, discrete periods, and varied (intended) audiences. In the early twentieth century, Tove would prefer medieval ballads, and she burst into tears upon hearing religious nineteenth-century poetry for the first time. By following these children, we have also been able to show how children would encounter and enjoy literary texts written and published in Danish in combination with translations or texts they heard or read in other languages. In short, books for children in the Nordic countries have always been a transnational phenomenon.

Across the centuries, children have also produced texts and media themselves, often in cooperation with peers and adults. Friederike, Hans Christian, Ida, and Anton all initiated and placed themselves at the center of dramatic performances, even in plays of their own devising. Ida and her peers also communicated through letters, while children like Palle Huld and Ileana Holmboe in the twentieth century were encouraged to write and publish books. Children as co-creators and co-producers of texts – including television programs – became a core element in the 1968 ideology of childhood. Today, most Nordic children have access to means of production and publication through their computers.

When seeking access to texts and media, children often depend on adults. Friederike's father limited her access to further education, while Tove's mother taught her to read. Adults outside the family can also play an important role when opening their doors and libraries to less privileged children, like Hans Christian and Anton. Tove's clever, perceptive teacher helped to open a new world of books for her, while Jens Otto's teachers made his school a boring, unpleasant place. Other groups of adults who play key roles in the history of children's literature are the authors, translators, publishers, printers, and booksellers involved in producing and disseminating books for children. They have not been at the center of this account, but we have pointed to both continuities and changes in their work as well. Once, publishing books for children was a small niche in the book market. Later it became an important part of the publishing profile for a number of established publishing houses, and today it is sometimes a global business operating in an international market. In the bookshops of the late 1700s and early 1800s, customers would usually decide themselves how they wanted a book bound, and whether they wished to pay for colored illustrations. Later, publishers would design covers and other aspects of the physical books, while today it is once again possible to make a number of individual choices when buying books online.

Children's access to books and media in the Nordic countries – and thus their access to knowledge and experiences of art and popular culture – has also depended on public institutions. Since the 1730s, all children in Denmark have been expected to learn to read and receive basic (religious) education, but for centuries the differences in education and media access for rich and poor, for boys and girls, and for children in urban and rural settings remained considerable. From 1814 onwards, the ambition has been that all children have a right and an obligation to receive a basic education provided by the state, and twentieth-century reforms aimed to diminish the inequalities relating to gender and social background, although they were not always successful. Schools would often have small collections of books, but only with the public library acts of the twentieth century did libraries begin to provide general access to books for all children – first and foremost in the cities. The development of the welfare state played a very important part in continuously developing publicly run schools, libraries, and daycare institutions for young children, which integrated activities linked to books and media. While inequalities remain, and have been increasing since the 2000s, the shared media culture surrounding children in public institutions has, to some extent, meant a homogenization of childhoods.

Nevertheless, the history of welfare institutions does not exclusively represent progress in terms of increased access to media and literature. In recent decades the merging of Danish municipalities and the construction of larger libraries with more facilities have reduced the number of local libraries. From a child's perspective, being able to walk or cycle to a local library might be more important than having multiple facilities and up-to-date architecture available all in one place, but far from home. Digitial access has created new opportunities for children outside major towns and cities. However, increased attention to digital literacy and the integration of digital media in schools, libraries, and daycare centers have also led to concerns about the future role and importance of books and literature.

Across the centuries, books and media have been used to inform children and to educate and shape coming generations of future citizens. The questions of how such information should be imparted, how the author should address children, and not least what the content should be have been the subject of vehement discussions and profound changes – although here, too, clear continuities and complex chronologies are striking. First, there are the genres and styles of writing. In the eighteenth century, books and newspapers for children mixed fact and fiction, and children's literature was meant to educate, enlighten, and entertain at the same time. During the nineteenth century, fact and fiction were increasingly separated. The market for schoolbooks expanded, and for many publishers, textbooks for schools became, and remain, an important part of their production. When it comes to children's fiction, new genres regularly replace or are added to existing ones. For instance, poetry for children evolved in Denmark from the 1830s onwards under the influence of Romanticism, and it became an important genre in the shape of lyrics in songbooks and as accompanying text in the new picturebooks. Today, children experience poetry in new and old songs as well as in picturebooks. While novels for children did not exist in the 1770s, they began to appear in the second half of the nineteenth century, and the novel is still an immensely popular genre today. Opinions about whether children are attracted – or ought to be attracted – to realistic narratives or fantastical tales, including fairytales and fantasy, have varied and were much discussed over the centuries. During the debates of the 1970s about the necessity of confronting children with reality, few would have predicted that fantasy would once again become a dominant genre 30 years later.

Such debates are closely linked to changing views on childhood, and on what content children should encounter through literature. In the eighteenth century, the main focus was on the education of children as good Christians within a hierarchical, patriotic society, and the Christian doctrines had to be learned by heart. Closer to 1800, Enlightenment thinking gave rise to new content and new approaches, addressing children as potentially enlightened citizens and meaning more stories featuring children's lives and experiences. In the early decades of the 1800s, a new discourse framing children as individuals with special qualities, such as a connection to nature and the imagination, was introduced in and around children's literature. The nineteenth century also witnessed an increased focus on national identity and history, resulting in many children's books that addressed such topics and advocated traditional values, including in relation to gender roles. Building on ideas about children's autonomy, several twentieth-century authors developed and created new stories and genres, featuring independent children with agency, who would help shape a new and better world. At the same time, old classics and children's bibles were frequently reprinted and used as gifts. Close links between (changing) visions of the future and children's literature have always been present in children's books, as they are today.

For centuries, historical factors have interacted with children's texts and media to promote ideals of *Bildung* and citizenship. The contents of textbooks and of fiction reflect a relatively constant representation of the child as a patriotic citizen, especially during and after times of war, but it is also remarkable that since the late eighteenth century, children's texts and media have engaged in discussions of universalism and ideas related to world citizenship. Today, titles addressing global concerns such as immigration and climate change seem to reinforce this trend.

Denmark has served as our central example in this outline of children's books and reading cultures in the Nordic world. Specific historical contexts must often be taken into account when explaining changes and continuities in and around children's literature, and a number of differences do exist among the Nordic countries. However, many general characteristics and even quite specific phenomena have been shared across the Nordic region, and especially among the three Scandinavian countries, in terms of institutions and media; approaches to children and conceptions of childhood; literary genres and topics; and even specific titles and authors' oeuvres.

This book has sought to tread new ground in its descriptions of children's literature and media and their complex chronologies. Children as users and occasionally as producers of texts have been our point of departure in attempting to present new knowledge by combining approaches from literary history, book history, cultural history, and childhood studies. In this condensed form, our ambition was not to paint an exhaustive or comprehensive picture, but rather to open the eyes of the reader to greater variety, to new perspectives, and to surprising and thought-provoking elements in and around the multifaceted field of children's reading and media culture in the Nordic region.

Suggestions for further reading

Aasgaard, R. et al. (Eds.). (2018). *Nordic Childhoods 1700-1960: From Folk Beliefs to Pippi Longstocking*. Routledge.

Appel, C. & Christensen, N. (2017). Follow the Child, Follow the Books: Cross-Disciplinary Approaches to a Child-Centred History of Danish Children's Literature 1790-1850. *International Research in Children's Literature, 10*(2), 194-212.

Goga, N. et al. (Eds.). (2018). *Ecocritical Perspectives on Children's Texts and Cultures: Nordic Dialogues*. Springer International Publishing.

Strandgaard Jensen, H. (2017). *From Superman to Social Realism: Children's Media and Scandinavian Childhood*. John Benjamins.

References

Andersen, H. C. [1835]. Little Ida's Flowers. Translated by Jean Hersholt. https://andersen.sdu.dk/vaerk/hersholt/LittleIdasFlowers.html

Andersen, H. C. (2013). *My Fairy-Tale Life*. Translated by W. Glynn Jones. Dedalus.

Andersen, J. (2017). *Under bjælken. Et portræt af Kronprins Frederik*. Gyldendal.

Andersson, M. (2021). *Framtidens kvinnor. Mognad och medborgarskap i svenska flickböcker 1832-1921*. Makadam.

Andersson, M. & Druker, E. (Eds.). (2017). *Mångkulturell barn- och ungdomslitteratur*. Studentlitteratur.

Appel, C. (forthcoming). Translating, transforming, and targeting books for children. Author and publisher Morten Hallager as a transnational agent in late Enlightenment Denmark. In C. Appel et al. (Eds.).

Transnational Books for Children 1750-1900. John Benjamins.

Appel, C. et al. (forthcoming). Children's books and childhood reading in eighteenth- and nineteenth-century Denmark: Memoirs and autobiographies as sources for children's media repertoires. *Mémoires du livre / Studies in Book Culture*.

Appel, C. & Christensen, N. (2017). Follow the Child, Follow the Books: Cross-Disciplinary Approaches to a Child-Centred History of Danish Children's Literature 1790-1850. *International Research in Children's Literature, 10*(2), 194-212.

Appel, C. & Coninck-Smith, N. (Eds.). (2013-2015). *Dansk skolehistorie. Hverdag, vilkår og visioner gennem 500 år* (Vols. 1-5). Aarhus Universitetsforlag.

Baden Staffensen, K. (2018). Rochows mange børnevenner. *Uddannelseshistorie 2018*, 99-118.

Barfod, F. (1836). *Poetisk Læsebog for Børn og barnlige Sjæle, til Brug saavel i Skolen som i Huset*. Bianco Luno.

Bertelsen, K. et al. (1981). Bare man eksisterer påvirker man jo andre! Interview med Helga Mollerup. In *Børn, bøger, biblioteker*, 86-94. Bibliotekscentralen.

Birkeland, T. et al. (Eds.). (2005/2018). *Norsk barnelitteraturhistorie*. Samlaget.

Bjørkøy, A. & Kaasa, J. (forthcoming). The Journey of "Lille Alvilde": The Fluid Life of a Children's Classic. In C. Appel et al. (Eds.). *Transnational Books for Children 1750-1900*. John Benjamins.

Bluitgen, K. (2006). *Koranen og profeten Muhammeds liv*. Høst.

Borring Olesen, T. & Poulsen, B. (Eds.). (forthcoming). *A History of Denmark*. Aarhus University Press.

Brandes, G. (1905). *Levned*. Gyldendal.

Brembeck, H. et al. (Eds.). (2004). *Beyond the competent child. Exploring contemporary childhoods in the Nordic welfare societies*. Roskilde University Press.

107

Brodersen, J., & Engsig Eskildsen, P. (2020). *Vi ændrer verden. 30 historier om modige børn.* Høst.

Brun, F. (1824). *Wahrheit aus Morgenträumen und Idas ästhetische Entwickelung.* Sauerländer.

Brüggemann, T. & Ewers, H. H. (1982). *Handbuch zur Kinder- und Jugendliteratur: von 1750 bis 1800.* Metzler.

Bunge, M. J. (2018). "A Plain and Cheerful, Active Life on Earth": Children, Education, and Faith in the Works of N.F.S. Grundtvig (1783–1872, Denmark). In R. Aasgaard et al. (Eds.). *Nordic Childhoods 1700–1960: From Folk Beliefs to Pippi Longstocking.* 111–130. Routledge.

Caën, A. (1850). *Prøven paa Slaget ved Fredericia. Original Børnevaudeville i 1 Act.* Th. Gandrup.

Campe, J. H. (1814). *Robinson den Yngre. En lærerig og med tvende Kobbere forsynet Morskabsbog for Børn. Oversat efter den ottende Udgave af Plesner.* J. S. Schultz.

Campe, J. H. (1819). *Robinson der jüngere. Ein Lesebuch für Kinder* (13th ed.). Verlag der Schulbuchhandlung. https://publikationsserver.tu-braunschweig.de

Capshaw, K. (2021). Race. In P. Nel et al. (Eds.), *Keywords for Children's Literature*, 164–168. New York University Press.

Chakravarty, D. & Mortensen, M. (2014). *De danske kvinders historie.* Systime.

Christensen, N. (2003). *Den danske billedbog 1950–1999: teori, analyse, historie.* Roskilde Universitetsforlag.

Christensen, N. (2012). *Videbegær. Oplysning, børnelitteratur, dannelse.* Aarhus Universitetsforlag.

Christensen, N. (2021). Agency. In P. Nel et al. (Eds.), *Keywords for Children's Literature*, 10–13. New York University Press.

Christensen, V. T. (2019). *Pisa 2018. En sammenfatning.* Vive.

Coninck-Smith, N. de (2021). Barndom i bevægelse. In M. Dael et al. (Eds.), *Børnekultur i Danmark 1945–2020*, 20–40. Gad.

Coninck-Smith, N. de & Appel, C. (2021). 500 years of Danish school history: methodologies, agencies, and connecting

narratives. *Paedagogica Historica.* https://doi.org/10.1080
/00309230.2021.1965174

Dansk. Fælles Mål (2019). Undervisningsministeriet.

Ditlevsen, T. (1975). *Tove Ditlevsen om sig selv.* Gyldendal.

Druker, E. & Kümmerling-Meibauer, B. (Eds.). (2015). *Children's
literature and the avantgarde.* John Benjamins.

Fass, P. S. et al. (Eds.). (2004). *Encyclopedia of children and
childhood in history and society* (Vols. 1-5). Macmillan.

Faye Jacobsen, A. (2017). Children's Rights and Duties:
Snapshots into the History of Education and Child
Protection in Denmark. In R. Aasgaard et al. (Eds.),
*Nordic Childhoods 1700-1960: From Folk Beliefs to Pippi
Longstocking*, 91-107. Routledge.

Field, H. (2019). *Playing with the Book. Victorian Movable
Picture Books and the Child Reader.* University of
Minnesota Press.

Genette, G. (1997). *Paratexts. Thresholds of Textuality of
Interpretation.* Cambridge University Press.

Goga, N. et al. (Eds.). (2018). *Ecocritical Perspectives on
Children's Texts and Cultures: Nordic Dialogues.* Springer
International Publishing.

Gold, C. (1996). *Educating Middle Class Daughters. Private Girls
Schools in Copenhagen 1790-1820.* Museum Tusculanum.

Goldman, P. (2013). The History of Illustration and its
Technologies. In M. Suarez & H. R. Woudhuysen (Eds.),
The Book. A Global History, 231-244. Oxford University
Press.

Graff, H. et al. (Eds.). (2009). *Understanding Literacy in its
Historical Contexts.* Nordic Academic Press.

Gubar, M. (2016). The Hermeneutics of Recuperation: What a
Kinship-Model Approach to Children's Agency Could
do for Children's Literature and Children's Literature
Studies. *Jeunesse, 8*(1), 291-310.

Gustafsson, H. (2017). *Nordens historia: En europeisk region
under 1200 år.* Studentlitteratur.

Hallberg, K. (1996). *Den svenska bilderboken och modernismens folkhem*. Stockholms Universitet.

Hansen, J. V. & Scheutz, S. (Eds.). (2021). *Medieudviklingen 2020*. Danmarks Radio. English edition: https://www.dr.dk/om-dr/about-dr/media-development-2010-2020

Hasebrink, U. & Hepp, A. (2017). How to research cross-media practices? Investigating media repertoires and media ensembles. *Convergence, 23*(4), 362–377.

Henkel, A. Q. (2021). In-Between. Intermedial understanding and analysis of children's literature: Exemplified by the digital story NORD (2018). *Nordic Journal of ChildLit Aesthetics, 12*(1), 1–15.

Henkel, A. Q. et al. (forthcoming). *Læsere mellem medier. Silkeborgundersøgelsen. Rapport om læse- og mediepraksis blandt børn i 6. og 8. klasse.*

Heikkilä-Halttunen, P. (2012). Idyllic childhood, jagged youth: Finnish books for children and young people meet the world. In L. Kirstinä (Ed.), *Nodes of contemporary Finnish literature*, 136–151. Finnish Literature Society.

Heywood, S. & Strandgaard Jensen, H. (2018). Exporting the Nordic Children's '68. The global publishing scandal of The Little Red Schoolbook. *Barnboken, 41*. https://doi.org/10.14811/clr.v41i0.332

Hogsnes, H. et al. (2020). Litteraturens og høytlesingens plass og hensikt i nasjonale policydokumenter for barnehagen og barnehagelærerutdanningen i Danmark, Finland, Norge og Sverige. *Barn, 4*, 15–33.

Huld, P. (1928). *Jorden rundt i 44 Dage*. Hasselbalch.

Ingemann, B. S. (1837). *Morgensange for Børn*. Andreas Seidelin.

James, A. & James, A. L. (2012). *Key concepts in childhood studies*. SAGE.

Jensen, C. (2021). *Equality in the Nordic World*. Aarhus University Press / The University of Wisconsin Press.

Jespersen, K. J. V. (2011). *A History of Denmark* (2nd ed.). Palgrave Macmillan.

Johansen, S. L. (2021). Münster's Inc. Children as influencers balancing celebrity, play and paychecks. In Ines de la Ville (Ed.), *Cultural and Creative Industries of Childhood and Youth. An interdisciplinary exploration of new frontiers*, 55–172. Peter Lang.

Johansson, E. (1981). The history of literacy in Sweden. In H. Graff (Ed.), *Literacy and Social Development in the West*, 156–182. Cambridge University Press.

Joosen, V. (2006). Cautionary Tales. In J. Zipes (Ed.), *The Oxford Encyclopedia of Children's Literature*, 269–270. Oxford University Press.

Juska-Bacher, B. et al. (Eds.). (forthcoming). *Learning to Read, Learning Religion: Catechism Primers in Europe from the 16th to the 19th Centuries*. John Benjamins.

Kaasa, J. S. (2019). "Saavel fra fjerne Lande som fra vort eget Hjem". Importert materiale i Billed-Magazin for Børn. In A. M. B. Bjørkøy et al. (Eds.), *Litterære verdensborgere. Transnasjonale perspektiver på Norsk bokhistorie 1519–1850*, 310–329. Nota Bene.

Kastberg. K. (1967). Skolebibliotekerne gennem tiderne. In J. Christiansen & P. Rønn Christensen (Eds.), *Skolebibliotekerne i Danmark,* 9–116. Gyldendal.

Klog, S. (2018). Glæden ved et liv med bøger. Interview med Rachel Röst. https://www.blivklog.dk/glaeden-ved-et-liv-med-boger/

Krabbe, N. (1996). *Music in Copenhagen. Studies in the musical life of Copenhagen in the 19th and 20th centuries*. C. A. Reitzel.

Krag, J. (1969). *Ung mand fra trediverne*. Gyldendal.

Kristjánsdóttir, D. (2015). *Bókabörn Íslenskar barnabókmenntir verða til*. Bókmennta- og listfræðastofnun Háskólaútgáfan.

Lindgren, A. (1945). *Pippi Langstrump*. Rabén & Sjögren.

Lindgren, A. (1981). *Ronja rövardotter*. Rabén & Sjögren.

Lindkvist, L. (2018). Rights for the World's Children: Rädda Barnen and the Making of the UN Convention on the

Rights of the Child. *Nordic Journal of Human Rights,*
36(3), 287–303.

Linkis, S. (2019). *Memory, Intermediality, and Literature:*
Something to hold on to. Routledge.

Lov om statsunderstøttede Biblioteker. (1921). Statens
Bibliotekstilsyn.

Lundtofte, T. (2021). Lidt om dillermænd, leg og Ole Lund
Kirkegaard. https://www.kommunikationsforum.dk/
artikler/DR-s-nye-serie-John-Dillermand

Lønborg Jensen, M. & Moe, L. (1924). *Min første Bog* (5th ed.).
Gyldendalske Boghandel og Nordisk Forlag.

Mansour, N. & Martin, M. (2020) What Can Danish Multicultural
Children's Literature and African American Children's
Literature Learn from Each Other? Literary Histories in
Dialogue. *Barnboken,* 43, http://dx.doi.org/ 10.14811/clr.
v43i0.503

Maza, S. (2020). The Kids Aren't All right: Historians and the
Problem of Childhood. *American Historical Review,*
124(4), 1261–1285.

Mygind, S. (2019). *Børnelitteratur i transmedial bevægelse.*
Aarhus Universitet.

Mygind, S. & Poulsen. J. (2018). Det litterære computerspil. In
T. Rye Andersen et al. (Eds.), *Litteratur mellem medier.*
Aarhus Universitetsforlag.

Nel, P. (2017). *Was the cat in the hat black? The hidden racism*
of children's literature, and the need for diverse books.
Oxford University Press.

Nielsen, A. (1894). *Landsbyliv i Trediverne. Barndomsminder.*
Milo'ske Boghandels Forlag.

Nielsen, E. (1986). Eventyrenes modtagelseskritik. In E. Dal
(Ed.), *H.C. Andersens Eventyr VI. Bemærkninger m.m.*
Textkritik. Modtagelseskritik, 121–230. C.A. Reitzel.

Nielsen, H. (1960). *Folkebibliotekernes forgængere: oplysning,*
almue- og borgerbiblioteker fra 1770erne til 1834. Dansk
Bibliografisk Kontor.

Nikolajeva, M. & Scott, C. (2001). *How picturebooks work*. Garland Publishing.

Oehlenschläger, A. (1816). *Eventyr af forskiellige Digtere. I–II*. Gyldendal.

O'Malley, A. (2012). *Children's literature, popular culture and Robinson Crusoe*. Palgrave Macmillan.

Ommundsen, Å. M. (2015). Who are These Books For? Controversial Picturebooks and the Question of Audience. In J. Evans (Ed.), *Challenging Picturebooks. Creative and Critical Responses to Visual Texts*. Routledge.

Ommundsen, Å. M. (2021). Taboo. In Nel et al. (Eds.), *Keywords for Children's Literature*, 178–181. New York University Press.

Rasmussen, T. (1787). *ABC*. P. H. Höeke.

Reinholdt Hansen, S. (2018). *Børns læsevaner 2017 – overblik og indblik*. Tænketanken Fremtidens Biblioteker.

Sareen, M. & Ditlev, N. (2015). *Manu*. Politiken.

Sigvaldi, O. (Ed.). (1968–1971). *Hindbærbrus og Kragetæer*. Sigvaldis Forlag.

Skyggebjerg, A. (2008). *Den historiske roman for børn. Teori, udvikling og analyse*. Dansklærerforeningen.

Starup, M. & Naur Jensen, J. (Eds.). (2020). *Bogen og litteraturens vilkår 2020. Bogpanelets årsrapport*. Slots- og Kulturstyrelsen.

Steffensen, A. & Weinreich, T. (2001). *Den dyrebare tid. De 14–15 åriges læsevaner*. Roskilde Universitetsforlag.

Stockmann. D. et al. (2000). *The book trade in Finland: From author to reader – support measures and development in the book trade*. Ministry of Education.

Strandgaard Jensen, H. (2017). *From Superman to Social Realism: Children's Media and Scandinavian Childhood*. John Benjamins.

Stybe, V. (1983). *Fra billedark til billedbog*. Arnold Busck.

Svensson, S. (2018). *Barnavänner och skolkamrater: Svenska barn- och ungdomstidningar 1766-1900 sedda mot en internationell bakgrund.* Carlssons.

Tellgren, C. (1982). *På barnens bokmarknad: utgivningen av barn- och ungdomslitteratur i Sverige 1966-1975.* Bonniers.

Thrane, L. (2015). *Vildfugl og verdensborger. Tretten fortællinger om Estrid Ott og hendes tid.* U Press.

Vogel, H. (1981) *Bilderbogen, Papiersoldat, Würfelspiel und Lebensrad. Volkstümliche Graphik für Kinder aus fünf Jahrhunderten.* Edition Papp.

Wegener, A. (2021). *Karin Michaëlis' Bibi Books. Producing, Rewriting, Reading and Continuing a Children's Fiction Series, 1927-1953.* Frank & Timme.

Weinreich, T. (2006). *Historien om børnelitteratur. Dansk børnelitteratur gennem 400 år.* Branner og Korch.

Weinreich, T. (2015). *Den socialistiske børnebog.* Roskilde Universitetsforlag.

Weld, S. P. (2014). *Voiceless Vanguard. The Infantilist Aesthetic of the Russian Avant-Garde.* Northwestern University Press.

Westin, B. (2004). The Nordic Countries. In P. Hunt (Ed.), *The Routledge Companion to Children's Literature*, 1056-1167. Routledge.

Westin, B. (2014). *Tove Jansson: Life, Art, Words.* Sort Of Books.

Whalley, J. & Chester, T. (1988). *A History of Children's Book Illustration.* Murray.

Widhe, O. (2021). The Politics of Autobiography in Katarina Taikon's Katitzi Series. *Children's Literature, 49.* https://doi.org/10.1353/chl.2021.0005

Winge, M. (1976). *Dansk børnelitteratur 1900-1945 med særligt henblik på børneromanen.* Gyldendal.

Winther, C. & Rørby, M. (1846). *Fem og tyve Billeder for smaa Børn.* Reitzel.

Zweigbergk, E. von (1965). *Barnboken i Sverige 1750-1950.* Rabén & Sjögren.

Ørjasæter, K. & Johnsen, L. (2021). *Kan vi måle graden av litterært mangfold?* https://barnebokinstituttet.no/aktuelt/kan-vi-male-graden-av-litteraert-mangfold/

Øster, A. (2002). Sunde og gode bøger for ungdommen – Mathilde Groos' fortællinger 1885-1901. *Nedslag i børnelitteraturforskningen, 3*, 139-164.

Øster, A. (Ed.). (2016). *Den nordiske børnebog.* Høst.